MW01050177

WILD TURKEY
COUNTRY

Text and Photography by
Lovett E. Williams, Jr.

Photographs by
Gary W. Griffen

NORTHWORD PRESS
Minnetonka, Minnesota
www.howtobookstore.com

© Lovett E. Williams, Jr., 1991
Photography © Lovett E. Williams, Jr. and Gary Griffen, 1991

NorthWord Press
5900 Green Oak Drive
Minnetonka, MN 55343
1-800-328-3895
www.howtobookstore.com

All rights reserved. No part of this work covered by the copyrights here-on may be reproduced or used in any form or by any means—graphic, electronic or mechanical, including photocopying, recording, taping of information on storage and retrieval systems—without the prior written permission of the publisher.

The copyright on each photograph in this book belongs to the photo-grapher, and no reproductions of the photographic images contained herein may be made without the express permission of the photographer.

Designed by Mary Schafer

Library of Congress Cataloging-in-Publication Data
Williams, Lovett E.
    Wild turkey country / Lovett E. Williams, Jr.
        p.   cm.
    Includes bibliographical references.
    ISBN 1-55971-206-6
    1. Wild turkeys. I. Title.
QL696.G254W54   1991
598' .619--dc20   90-24080

Printed in China

10 9 8 7 6 5 4 3

CONTENTS

Lovett Edward Williams, Jr., is a sixth generation Floridian, born May 10, 1935 in Perry, Florida. He holds a Bachelor of Science in zoology from Florida State University in Tallahassee and a Master of Science in Wildlife Management, from Auburn University in Alabama. He went on to the University of Florida in Gainesville for his Ph.D. in Wildlife Ecology.

Much of **Wild Turkey Country** is the result of studies Williams performed for his master's thesis, *Analysis of Wild Turkey Field Sign: An Approach to Census* and for his Ph.D. thesis, *Reproductive Behavior and Performance of the Female Florida Wild Turkey.*

Although turkeys have dominated Williams' career, he has served as a navigator and port security officer for the U.S. Coast Guard, wildlife consultant and president of Florida Wildlife Services, Inc., and vice president of Old Masters Publishers, Inc., publishers of rare, out-of-print hunting titles.

His other posts have included that of field editor for *The Turkey Hunter* magazine, president of Real Turkeys Publishers, under whose auspices he has self-published several books, and director of marketing and sales for Real Turkey audio cassettes, books and hunting products.

Currently, Williams remains a freelance writer and photographer on wildlife and outdoor subjects, a topic he also covers in educational seminar presentations. He is predominantly occupied with the promotion of his mail order business and hunting lodge, of which he is co-owner. He also performs land and harvest management activities on the 14,000 acre hunting area leased by the lodge, and conducts nature tours on the land.

Professional awards garnered by Williams include, among others: the Henry S. Mosby Memorial Award from the National Wild Turkey Federation, for contributions to research and management of the wild turkey' Wildlife Conservationist of the Year (1977) from the Florida Wildlife Federation; and several awards of Excellence for technical publications by the Wildlife Society's Southeastern Section.

This is not surprising, as Williams is a veteran in the field of technical publications in his specialization, the wild turkey. He has authored 33 scientific papers on all aspects of the wild turkey's natural history, 41 educational magazine articles and currently does a question-and-answer column for *The Turkey Hunter* magazine. He has also published articles on many other non-turkey wildlife topics.

His other books include *The Book of the Wild Turkey,* a general title on life history, distribution and hunting of the species (1981, Winchester Press); *The Voice and Vocabulary of the Wild Turkey,* a semi-technical account of wild turkey vocalizations based on his large collection of audio recordings obtained during field research (1984); and *Studies of the Wild Turkey,* a scientific report on previously unpublished field and laboratory research findings (1988, University Presses of Florida).

He lives with his wife Pam and their two daughters in an old-fashioned Florida "Cracker" house in Gainesville, Florida, which they share with a small menagerie of farm animals and fowl.

Opening spread photo courtesy the author.

Gary W. Griffen holds a Master of Arts in Communication, specializing in film and magazines, from Syracuse University, New York. He and his wife, Marcia, produce award-winning films for such entities as Discovery, National Geographic, foreign television and home video. Their wildlife and nature photographs have been published in national magazines, books and calendars.

Their film, *America's Wild Turkey*, earned the distinction of Best Wildlife Documentary at the International Wildlife Film Festival and first place from the Outdoor Writer's Association of America and Chevron, U.S.A.

Another film, *Whitetail Country*, garnered a Cindy Award; the New York Festival's Bronze Award; and a Merit Award from the International Wildlife Festival.

The Griffens won Best of Festival at the National Outdoor Film Festival with their showing of *The Living Landscape*. The Association for Conservation Information also recognized this film with a Gold Award, as did Intercom 85 by presenting it with a Hugo.

Their documentary *Guarding our Living Environment* won Best Ecology Documentary at the National Outdoor Film Fesitval; a Bronze Award from the Houston International Film Festival; and a Gold Award from the Association for Conservation Information, as well as a Cindy Award.

Their photographs in **Wild Turkey Country** are the product of months of patient waiting for these wild and crafty birds to come before their cameras. Most of the photographs were taken during the filming of *America's Wild Turkey*. All depict wild birds in free-roaming situations. The captions for all photographs by the Griffens were provided by the photographers.

Gary Griffen photo

Following Page — *A primary feather lying on the floor of a pine forest. Toms molt in spring. (Gary Griffen photo)*

PREFACE

My experience with the wild turkey began with awe some 30 years ago when I was a young hunter. I had hunted small game near my northern Florida home during my early teen years without seeing a wild turkey. Then, early one cool, fall morning, I met an old woodsman in the river swamp. He carried a gobbler he had just shot. Flushed with excitement, I searched for evidence of the large birds after the old man departed, and found a large tail feather — like one from an old-fashioned turkey feather duster. The brown tip confirmed the feather was from a wild turkey. That day was the beginning of an enduring relationship between the wild turkey and me.

As a wildlife biologist I have worked with many species of wildlife and have affection for them all, but the wild turkey will always be a favorite. I am not alone in that fascination. The wild turkey has deeply intrigued almost everyone who has ever become acquainted with it, and the species has a large following today.

The wild turkey is a finely tuned product of nature — forged, shaped, and polished by the same forces that made us all. Evolution aims at perfection, but such perfection is never fully realized. In an evolutionary sense, what works today may not work tomorrow, so the wild turkey is always changing genetically to meet the challenges presented by its unstable environment. This has created considerable variation in the physical and behavioral features of the turkey. These differences did not come about haphazardly — variation is an important characteristic of the species. All turkeys do not appear or act exactly the same. I can promise that.

In *Wild Turkey Country*, I try to depict the turkey in a way that will appeal to readers already acquainted with it as well as those who are not. I have, by necessity, completed this portrait with a broad brush because there is so much more to tell than can be covered in one small book. Anybody who seeks more detail or has more interest in the scientific basis of the information presented may want to read my other books, *Studies of the Wild Turkey in Florida, The Voice and Vocabulary of the Wild Turkey,* and *The Book of the Wild Turkey,* and those papers and other books cited in them. (Refer to the suggested readings in the back of this book.)

Many of the photographs on these pages were made at Fisheating Creek, in Glades County, Florida, where I conducted field studies for many years with my colleague David H. Austin while we were both employed by the Florida Game and Fresh Water Fish Commission. Together we now own and manage a lodge on a large leased tract at Fisheating Creek where healthy populations of Florida wild turkeys live and are photographed, recorded, hunted, and greatly admired and appreciated.

Most of the photographs are of Florida turkeys and there is naturally a Florida wild turkey bias because of my years of study of these populations. Still, I have also studied and hunted the eastern wild turkey and have read extensively about the other subspecies and have tried to include as much information as possible about turkeys everywhere. There is but one species of wild turkey. The geographic differences in populations from place to place are not significant.

I enjoy telling the wild turkey story. I hope you enjoy reading it.

Lovett E. Williams, Jr.
Gainesville, Florida
May 13, 1990

INTRODUCTION

I stopped on the bank in a sharp bend of the creek to listen to the sounds of the swamp. The monotonous call of a chuck-will's-widow drifted in from the hill outside the swamp and was abruptly displaced by the hooting of a family of barred owls almost overhead. As the echoes faded, a night heron, by then finished with its night of foraging, squawked acknowledgment of the faint glow in the eastern sky.

Where I stood on the floor of the swamp, it was still dark. I could barely see the whiteness of a lichen on a gum tree a few feet away. As the barred owls hooted again, I moved on in the darkness toward my destination deeper in the swamp. I was there to stalk a flock of adult gobblers and determine their roosting site and the time of their leaving the roost.

As I moved eastward across a small opening, I could barely make out the skyline of the swamp ahead. From the upper limbs, small plumes of Spanish moss pointed like hermits' beards toward the ground. Dark round forms of cardinal airplants that dotted the limbs were silhouetted against the faint sky. My attention was suddenly brought back to ground level by the sound of a large animal — probably a deer — running across the opening and into the woods. As the noise faded in the distance, something, probably an otter, splashed softly in the creek.

Besides the sounds I could hear and the few images I could see, there was the pungent smell of yesterday's woods fire. The odor had come to the swamp on smoke from the prairie with the late afternoon wind. The scent had settled in the swamp overnight.

I could feel the humidity of the swamp's vapor. I knew it was beginning to condense into a thin haze that would be visible in the first morning light. I also knew I would soon be able to see the thin fog rising like steam from the black surface of Fisheating Creek as it drifted lazily upstream on the gentle breeze. The sky continued to grow lighter with a faint pink glow as morning came sneaking into the swamp.

My course carried me back into the cypress woods. Behind me, in the edge of the opening, a male cardinal sounded his melodic territorial song. A little farther along he was joined by two Carolina wrens that warbled their own claim to a piece of the swamp. An owl hooted again and was answered from farther down the creek. In the distance, a tufted titmouse called. This daybreak sounded like any other pre-dawn morning in a Florida swamp.

As the light continued to grow stronger, the dark knees of cypress trees became visible, pointing upward from the moist ground. Moments later, a spider's web, not a yard away and silvered with beads of morning dew, also became distinct. The dark spider in its center was motionless. I ducked to move under it and stopped again to listen and plan my course through the swamp.

A humming moth — perhaps a sphinx — hovered near my ear for an instant, as one often does just before sunrise in the creek swamp, and I could hear an early-flying flock of white ibis swishing overhead, alternately winging and gliding above the swamp in a wavering "V" formation. They were headed for their morning feeding grounds. A pair of sandhill cranes rattled and bugled their duet in a distant glade and half the woodpeckers in the swamp, namely the males, were drumming their

A woods fire. (Photo courtesy the author).

territorial tattoos on hollow trees. The chorus of night frogs had nearly stopped. A dozen white-eyed vireos and parula warblers had joined the morning throng to take up the slack. A red-shouldered hawk left its perch in a loblolly bay tree and winged and glided through the thick morning air, sounding its shrill call.

A few more steps brought me to my destination in a heavy growth of ferns. On one side was a decaying cypress log that must have been a thousand years growing and at least a hundred years on the ground among the ferns and mosses. The old cypress had been down so long that the canopy had closed overhead and there was no evidence of a vacancy in the over story. Just outside the swamp, not 200 yards away, was an Indian burial mound that I had often passed in my work with the turkeys. I wondered how many of the now-extinct Calusa Indians had seen the huge cypress tree alive and whether any had stood where I did after it was down.

There was a large oval hole on the upper side of the log. It must have been made by a large woodpecker when the tree was alive and standing. I wondered if the hole could have been made by an ivory-billed woodpecker. Whatever made it, the hole had been the home of no telling how many generations of different animals over the many lifetimes it stood in the swamp. Behind me was the dead tree's broken stump with fresh raccoon sign all about.

In summer, the normal water level would be up to my chest. This was the dry season, however, and I could stand in the swamp on dry feet. The morning light was almost strong enough for me to see everything around me. I had arrived at the roosting place in time.

From a limb halfway up a towering cypress tree, there was a loud crack of a brittle limb and the sound of wings in the wind. A large black bird, the source of the sounds, sailed through the trees not 30 feet overhead and landed. Then another great bird landed beside the first and two more sailed to the ground beyond.

The four wild turkey gobblers stood motionless for a moment, their reddish heads erect and listening. Their blackish-brown plumage made them difficult to see against the cypress buttresses in the dim light. Across the creek a flock of hen turkeys cackled loudly and left their roost. In a few more weeks the sound of hens would make the gobblers think of mating, and the tops of their heads would turn suddenly white and their necks red. But it was still late winter, too early for that, and the old gobblers paid no attention to the sounds.

Sunlight was touching the tops of the tallest trees now. The gobblers turned their heads to survey the woods ahead, then strode slowly through the cypress knees and out of the swamp to spend the day in the oak hammocks on higher ground.

Following a late winter snowstorm, a tom exhibits the alertness that will intensify with the coming of the spring mating season by taking up a vigilant post in a roost tree. (Gary Griffen photo)

Following page — Woods soon after a fire. (Photo courtesy the author)

The major external features of the wild turkey's body:
A) Beard B) Upper tail coverts C) Lower tail coverts D) Primary wing feathers E) Speculum F) Secondary wing feathers G) Tarsus
H) Tail (Gary Griffen Photo)

MEET THE WILD TURKEY

Ad ... leaving their roost
th ... stand nearly four feet
ta ... and are among the
l ...

... bler" because of his
... dark, glossy, metallic
... ddish, and greenish
... own and his head color
... the winter. The colors
... however, when mood
... obbler's bright red, white,
... lors tell receptive hens
that the male is ready for mating. The same colors tell
adversaries when he is ready for fighting. His head can
change colors quickly.

Male birds of species that have feathered heads must
replace part of their plumage before the mating season
and grow a "nuptial plumage" to advertise their sexual
maturity. A plumage change usually takes at least a
month, but the turkey gobbler's bare head can change
colors in a matter of seconds. This allows the bird to
communicate not only his adulthood but also his
immediate mood, in an unmistakable display of color.
Certain other bird species have bare skin that changes
colors during their mating seasons. I doubt, however,
that any can change their mood colors more quickly
than can the wild turkey.

The small, smooth bumps on the turkey's head and
neck are called "caruncles." The "snood" is the slender
appendage that arises from the top of the bill and
dangles beside it when the gobbler is sexually excited
in spring, is fighting, or is overheated by warm weather
or exercise.

The wild turkey's lower leg, called the *tarsometatarsus*
is scaly and unfeathered. The turkey poult's leg is flesh-
colored when it emerges from its eggshell but becomes
darker with age as a pigment called melanin is
deposited to toughen the paper-thin scales. Later in the
summer, a reddish tissue layer develops under the
scales of the young turkey's legs, but the color is partially
masked by the blackish melanin in the scales
themselves. As the growing scales become thicker and
tougher with age, less melanin is needed and less is
deposited. By fall, some of the reddish color of the
underlying pigment shows through. There is still
considerable melanin in the scales of a young fall turkey,
making its legs appear darker than the legs of adults
whose clear scales permit the red to show through
brightly. By the time the turkey is one year old, there
is no more melanin in the scales and the turkey's leg
is red.

There are no differences between the sexes in leg
color and no known geographic differences. The
domestic turkey, however, has legs that are brown, black,
or gray, rather than red.

Like the male domestic chicken and the pheasants,
close relatives of the turkey, the gobbler has sharp spurs
on the scaly part of his lower legs. The spurs are used
in fighting. The domestic chicken has wattles that
dangle under each side of the chin, but the wild turkey

*Page 13 — Drab forest surroundings are brightened by this healthy,
mature gobbler displaying all his springtime glory. The distinctive head
coloration signals to receptive hens his readiness for mating. (Gary
Griffen photo)*

Pages 14-15 — (Gary Griffen photo)

A neutral pink during most of the summer, a gobbler's head coloration changes in spring to a complex pattern of bright red, white and bluish-purple, indicating to hens a readiness for mating and to other toms a readiness for fighting. This color change takes place in a matter of seconds, allowing the bird to communicate not only his adulthood, but also his immediate mood. (Gary Griffen photo)

does not have wattles. The single fold of skin under the turkey's throat is called the *"dewlap."*

The male turkey has a hair-like "beard" that protrudes from the upper breast. The tip of the beard drags on the ground as he feeds, resulting in wear that prevents most beards from ever exceeding about 11 inches in length. A very few exceptional beards may reach 13 or 14 inches, however. The function of the beard is to enable other turkeys to distinguish adult from juvenile males at a glance. Annual shedding and regrowth of the beard would, of course, defeat that function. Although it does not look like a feather, the beard is a feather of a special type and the only one that is not shed in the annual molt.

A gobbler less than two years old is called a *"jake."* In fall and winter, jakes differ in physical features from adult males only in degree. They are lighter in weight, ranging from 9 to 15 pounds, duller in plumage sheen, and have short beards and blunt spurs. With its long legs, slim body, and snake-like neck, the fall jake exemplifies the streamlined physique for which the wild turkey is noted.

The female wild turkey is about half the weight of the male, tipping the scales from 6 to about 11 pounds, depending on age and physical condition. The hen's head is sparsely feathered and blue-gray colored throughout the year, regardless of her mood. Her snood is tiny. The bare skin of her head has a few caruncles that are sometimes pinkish colored.

One way to distinguish a gobbler from a hen is by the gobbler's beard, but that is not completely reliable because about four percent of the adult hens also have beards, and, occasionally, an adult gobbler will have no beard at all. The pink color of a male wild turkey's face, versus the blue-gray of the hen's, is a reliable way to determine sex in a bird in summer, fall, and winter. The difference is detectable even in turkeys as young as 16 weeks of age. During the mating season, the vivid bluish-purple, red, and white on the head and upper neck of the gobbler easily distinguishes him from a hen.

Leg spurs, which all normal male turkeys have, occur in a small proportion of the hens too. Hens that have

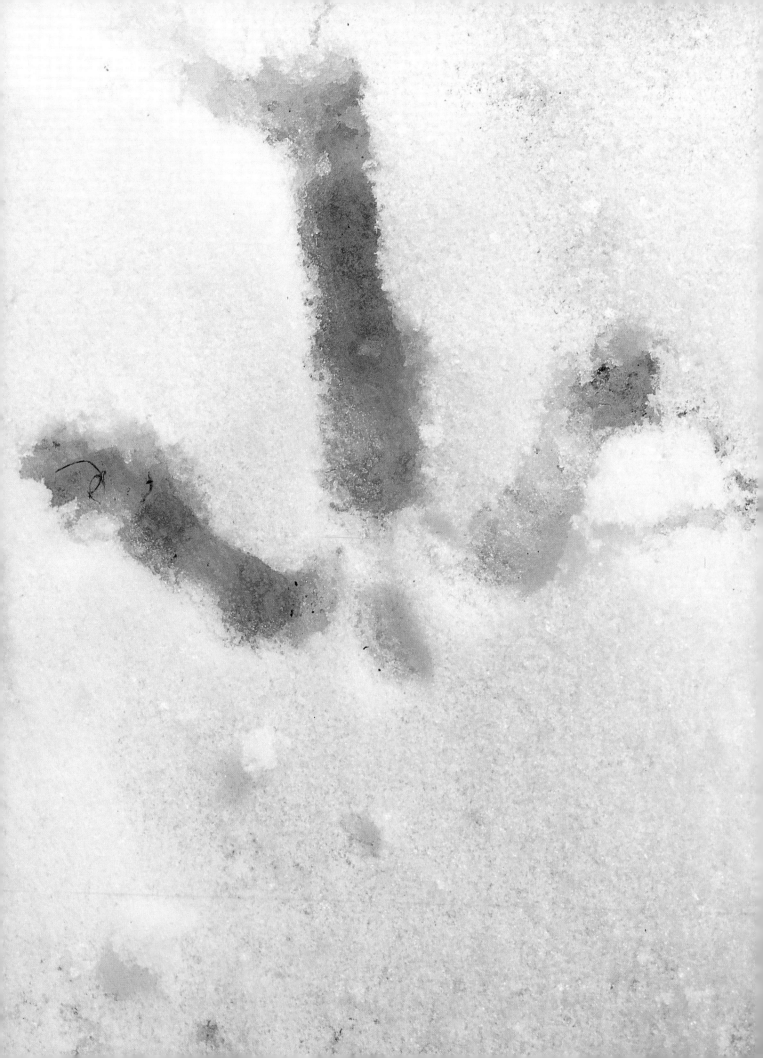

beards or spurs lay eggs and function as normal females. That is because these physical characteristics are controlled by genetics rather than by hormones. However, the plumage coloration of the hen is controlled by her hormones. If a hen's ovary is removed, she will assume a gobbler-like plumage on the following molt and, of course, cannot lay eggs. If a gobbler's testes are removed, he will continue to have the same plumage coloration as before. A small number of wild turkey hens have been found with perfect gobbler plumage features. Upon examination, it was found that their ovaries were severely damaged by some unknown agent, possibly an internal parasite.

One way to distinguish the sexes without seeing the bird is by the shape of their droppings. Males have long, straight or j-shaped droppings while hens have curled or bulbous droppings.

There are also differences in the sizes of the tracks made by hens and gobblers — the gobbler's track being larger, of course. Young turkeys have somewhat shorter and distinctively narrower toes than adults. Turkey scratching sign in the fall and winter forest litter is distinctive and, when freshly made, indicates a feeding area.

Not all wild turkeys have normal plumage coloration. Mutations and rare recessive genes account for a few specimens that are white, roan, speckled, and other colors. The same abnormal colors occur in domestic turkeys and in other wild birds and mammals. Contrary to popular opinion, unusual colors in the plumage of a wild turkey does not indicate an ancestry of domestic turkey strains.

Male and female turkeys hatch in equal proportions. Over a period of years, however, populations that are not hunted tend to build up higher numbers of males than females. This uneven proportion is the result of hens suffering higher rates of predation due to the hazards of nesting and poult rearing.

Young of most bird species, including the quails, grouses, pheasants, and other close relatives of the turkey, have three plumages during their first year of life. The rapidly growing young turkey has four. First there is a complete covering of soft natal down at the time of hatching. This down is soon replaced by the cryptic brown feathers of the juvenile plumage. The juvenile plumage in turn is replaced during the summer with a darker and more adult-like plumage. By the first winter of life that plumage, too, is replaced. The first winter plumage closely resembles that of the adult.

The process of feather replacement is called *molting*. Immediately after a feather is shed, a new feather begins to grow where the old one was located. If a feather is pulled out through accident, another like it begins to grow in its place. The pattern of molting is so systematic that the date of hatching can be determined up to the age of six months, with less than a five-day margin of error, by measuring the in-growing wing feathers.

Adult turkeys replace their entire plumage, except the beard of the male, once a year. The molt takes place in summer when body insulation is less important. Turkeys do not molt their feathers in large patches that would lay bare any spot of skin, and they do not experience a flightless period as many waterfowl do.

After a turkey reaches adulthood at about one and a half years of age, each annual plumage is exactly like the previous one. Therefore, it is not possible to determine the age of an adult turkey by its plumage features.

Despite their heavy weight, wild turkeys can rocket into the air from a standstill and zoom away at 55 miles per hour. They fatigue quickly, however, and their flight distances are short, seldom more than one-eighth of a mile. On foot, a turkey can easily outrun a man.

The turkey's eyesight is in some respects superior to man's and much different in its basic nature. Turkeys do not have to focus both eyes to see well. They can look in opposite directions simultaneously and can detect danger visually in a zone at least 300 degrees around

Page 19 — This tom has a double "beard" protruding from its upper breast. (Gary Griffen photo)

Page 20 — Turkey track in light snow. (Marcia Griffen photo)

The outer primary wing feather (far left) of an adult turkey is not as pointed or as brownish as that of a young bird. (Photo courtesy the author)

them — only a narrow sector directly behind a turkey's head remains unseen. By comparison, an owl can see only about 60 to 70 degrees. Birds in general cannot see as many color hues as can mammals, but turkeys do see colors, as is obvious by the way they react to the head and neck color changes of gobblers. Poults instinctively prefer to peck at green and yellow objects. White objects have less appeal. Turkeys also have outstanding hearing acuity, probably better than man's, but they have a poor sense of taste and little, if any, sense of smell.

The Turkey Subspecies

There are five subspecies of the American wild turkey, each differing from the others slightly in color and in certain other small physical features. The subspecies of southern Mexico, said to have been the progenitor of the domestic turkey, became extinct before the Spaniards arrived. This subspecies was killed out by the Indians near densely populated Mexico City (Leopold, 1959). The other five subspecies still occur in their original range in the United States, central and northern Mexico, southern Canada, and in new range where they have been stocked.

The wild turkey once occupied a vast range in the woodlands of the eastern United States from the Atlantic Ocean to the Great Plains, where it occurred only along tree-lined streams. In the East the turkey was limited in its northward range by harsh winter weather. The populations of the southern Rocky Mountains were isolated by treeless landscapes to the east, south, and west, and by occasional very harsh winter weather to the north. Populations once occurred throughout much of Mexico, but they did not occur farther south than Oaxaca (Leopold, 1972).

The wild turkey and its close relatives, including long-extinct forms, are all birds of the Western

Hemisphere. Not even a fossil of a turkey has ever been found anywhere else in the world.

The only other living turkey species in the world is the smaller and more colorful ocellated turkey of southern Mexico and Central America.

Eastern Wild Turkey
(*Meleagris gallopavo silvestris*)

The scientific name of the wild turkey species is *Meleagris gallopavo*. The term *silvestris*, which means "of the woodlands," is added to the species name to designate populations in the eastern U.S. (north of Florida) as a distinct subspecies.

The rump and tail margins of *silvestris* are brown. The primary wing feathers — those at the tip of the wing — have white and black bars that extend from the outer edge across each feather to the feather shaft. In *silvestris*, the white bars are as wide and prominent as the black. The secondary wing feathers — those between the primaries and the bird's body — also have prominent white bars and are edged in white, producing a whitish triangular area on each side of the back when the wings are closed.

Florida Wild Turkey
(*Meleagris gallopavo osceola*)

The name *osceola* designates populations of the Florida Peninsula as a distinct subspecies. The subspecies is named in honor of a 19th century Florida Seminole Indian leader.

The Florida subspecies is similar in feather markings to *silvestris* of the eastern U.S. except that more black and less white are seen in the primary and secondary wing feathers. Also the color tones throughout the plumage of the Florida wild turkey are slightly darker.

Following spread — These two pale turkey specimens (far left and middle) are examples of the "smoke gray" color aberration. (Photo courtesy the author)

In the Florida bird, the white wing feather bars are narrow, irregular and broken, and do not reach all the way to the feather shaft. The secondary wing feathers nearer the body are also dark on *osceola*. When the wing is folded on the back, these feathers do not form a whitish triangular patch as in *silvestris*.

Birds and mammals that live in humid climates are darker colored than examples of the same species living in more arid climates. The Florida turkey, living in humid, subtropical Florida, reflects this phenomenon. Featherwear is accelerated when feathers are damp. Nature prevents excessive wear in feathers and hair by reinforcing them with a substance called *melanin*. Melanin also happens to make feathers darker colored. It is the extra melanin in the feathers of the Florida wild turkey that makes it darker than the other subspecies.

The brown markings on the outer edge of the tail and rump (the large, upper tail coverts) distinguish both *osceola* and *silvestris* from the three western subspecies, which have the same feathers tipped with much lighter shades of tan, buff, and white. The tail margin is darkest in the Florida subspecies, next darkest in the eastern turkey, and progressively lighter in the Rio Grande, Merriams, and Goulds turkeys, in that order.

Rio Grande Wild Turkey
(*Meleagris gallopavo intermedia*)

The Rio Grande turkey is a bird of the southwestern U.S. and northeastern Mexico. The name *intermedia* reflects the opinion of the zoologist who named the subspecies that it is intermediate in appearance between the eastern and the western subspecies.

The Rio Grande turkey is distinguished from the eastern and Florida subspecies by having tail feathers and tail coverts tipped with light tan, rather than medium brown, and from the two other western subspecies by having a brownish tail margin that is

Page 26 — A Merriams wild turkey gobbler in Idaho. (Donald Jones photo courtesy the author)

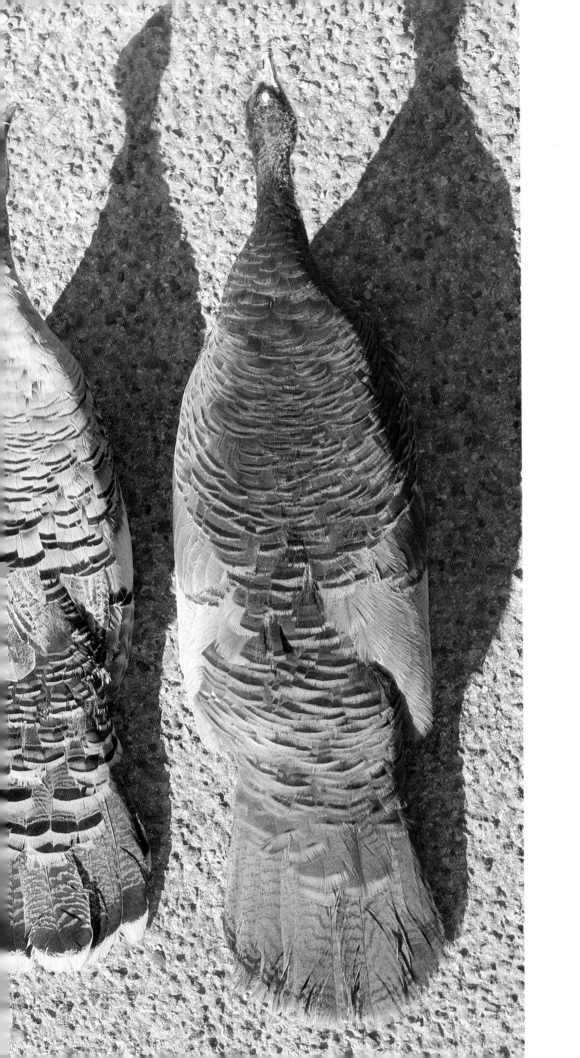

The tail margins and coverts of the Merriams wild turkey are light buff or near white. (Donald Jones photo courtesy the author)

darker than theirs.

The primary wing feathers of the Rio Grande turkey are not as black as the Florida turkey's, but, like the Florida turkey, its secondaries do not produce a conspicuous white triangular patch on the back when the wings are closed, as they do in the eastern subspecies.

Merriams Wild Turkey
(Meleagris gallopavo merriami)

Merriams wild turkey is a bird of the ponderosa pine foothills of the Rocky Mountains. It moves to higher altitudes in summer and back down in winter. The subspecies is named in honor of the zoologist C. Hart Merriam, from specimens taken in Veracruz, Mexico.

It has been successfully stocked north of its natural range in the Rockies and outside of the mountains in Nebraska and some other areas.

The Merriams wild turkey is distinguished from the eastern, Florida, and Rio Grande subspecies by the nearly white feathers of its lower back and tail margin. It closely resembles the Goulds turkey but the Merriams' tail margin is not quite as white nor is the light margin of the tail tip quite as wide as in the Goulds wild turkey.

Goulds Wild Turkey
(Meleagris gallopavo mexican)

The Goulds turkey, like the Merriams, is a bird of the mountains. A zoologist named Gould is credited with

Following spread — *The Merriams wild turkey of the southern Rocky Mountains has been successfully transplanted far north of its original range. (Donald Jones photo courtesy the author)*

2¼"

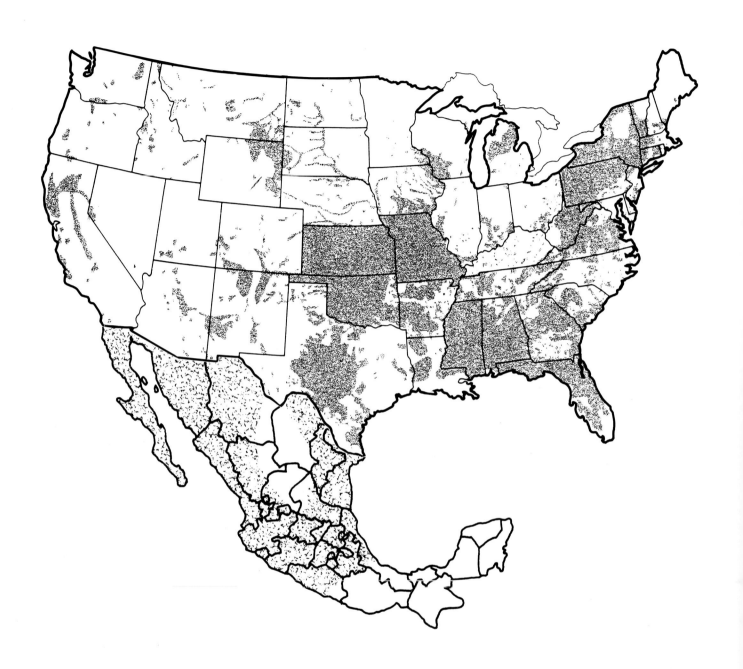

DISTRIBUTION RANGES
OF THE WILD TURKEY

describing the subspecies and his name has become the vernacular name for the subspecies. The original specimens were taken in northwestern Mexico in 1856. The Goulds wild turkey is the largest of the turkey subspecies.

The white tips of the upper tail coverts and the terminal band of the major tail feathers are wider than in the Merriams subspecies. The Goulds body plumage is said to have a somewhat bluish-green coloration.

In the U.S. there is only a small population of this subspecies along parts of the U.S.-Mexico border (Potter et al., 1985), but it is abundant in Mexico (Bland, 1986).

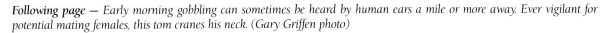

Following page — *Early morning gobbling can sometimes be heard by human ears a mile or more away. Ever vigilant for potential mating females, this tom cranes his neck. (Gary Griffen photo)*

RECENT HISTORY
OF THE WILD TURKEY

American Indians introduced European immigrants to beans, potatoes, tomatoes, corn, squash, pumpkins, tobacco, as well as other vegetable crops. They also introduced them to the domestic turkey — the only important domestic animal to originate in the Western Hemisphere.

Although the wild turkey is the progenitor of the domestic turkey, and although wild and domestic turkeys are of the same species, they are as different as night and day. Domestic turkeys have been molded in captivity through genetic selection to meet human requirements of profitable food conversion ratios, large size, plump breast, and white color. These human-inspired attributes are in direct opposition to the characteristics given the species by nature through the process of evolution. So, the domestic turkey we know today is a heavy, docile and noisy creature that is wholly dependent on man for its every need.

The turkey was domesticated by the Indians of Mexico and taken to Europe by the Spaniards. In Spain and in other European countries, turkeys were bred extensively in captivity. Later, domestic turkeys were carried from England to the British Colonies and thus re-entered the New World from Europe. This circuitous route may have contributed to some of the confusion about the correct name for the species. Nobody is sure how it came to be called "turkey."

Domestic turkey varieties come in various sizes and colors. The standard barnyard or "bronze" turkey still exhibits many of the color markings of the wild turkeys native to Mexico, where the species was probably domesticated about 2,000 years ago. The wild turkey of the eastern United States has never been domesticated.

Traditional wisdom says that the way to tell a domestic turkey from a wild one is by the white coloration on the outer edge of the tail feathers of the domestic variety. The wild variety supposedly has brown-tipped tail feathers, but this is true only of the eastern and Florida populations of wild turkey. Two of the western populations have white or nearly white tail margins similar to domestic turkeys. The color of the tail margin of the Rio Grande wild turkey is intermediate in shade between the eastern and domestic turkey.

The wild turkey has been an integral part of the wilderness of North America for thousands of years and an important food source for Native Americans. Evidence of this is seen in the many turkey bones found in Indian kitchen middens. Turkey feathers were used for Indian ceremonial dress and to fletch arrows, and turkeys are widely represented in Indian art.

Probably more than 40 million wild turkeys lived in North America when Columbus sailed. The vast hardwood forests of the eastern U. S. were intact then. The American chestnut was a dominant tree and an important source of wild turkey food. Hunting by the sparse Indian populations had little impact on wild turkey numbers.

During the period of early colonial settlement, the turkey earned a place in European-American culture and replaced the domestic goose as the main course for traditional family feasts. The U. S. Declaration of Independence and our Constitution were probably written with pens made from turkey feathers.

Although the wild turkey gobbler's head is a patriotic red, white, and blue and the species was highly revered by early Americans, it was not nominated for a place

on the National Emblem of the United States, as is widely believed. Benjamin Franklin, who is credited with that grand gesture, actually preferred a scene of Moses parting the Red Sea and Pharaoh's chariots being engulfed in the flood. Franklin's support of the wild turkey and his unfavorable comments about the bald eagle were written in a letter to his daughter Sarah in 1784 after the bald eagle had already been selected as our national bird (Smith, 1986).

As the eastern U. S. seaboard was becoming settled in the 1700s, a large and rapidly expanding commercial wild game market flourished. Wild turkeys and other game were being taken in large numbers by professional hunters and sold in the cities. Settlers themselves killed turkeys in large numbers for food.

The efficient weapons brought to the New World by the Europeans, coupled with the rapidly growing human population and the reckless American pioneer attitude toward natural resources, took their grievous toll. With a price on its head and market demand increasing, the wild turkey was almost eliminated from the eastern United States. By the 1940s, the species occupied only about 12 percent of its former range in the eastern U. S. and was not much better off in the West and South.

Deforestation, forest fires, and agriculture are often blamed for the demise of the wild turkey and other large game animals in the U. S., and some of these did have serious impacts on wildlife habitat. However, much habitat was still in good condition when the wild turkey and several other game species were eliminated from huge areas of their former range. Simply stated, the animals were excessively hunted as food or for their hides.

In 1730, dressed wild turkeys sold for 10 cents each in Massachusetts. Ninety years later, the price had risen to only 12 1/2 cents. As market hunting continued, though, wild turkey numbers began to dwindle and the law of supply and demand was felt. By the end of the

An alert young tom stands atop a stone wall amidst the changing colors of autumn, when large shifts in home range occur. (Gary Griffen photo)

market hunting era, wild turkeys sold for 25 cents a pound in New York City and three dollars for a large bird (Schorger, 1966).

The American conscience did not awaken to the plight of its wildlife resources until the early 1900s. By then, it was too late for the passenger pigeon, heath hen, and the Labrador duck — they were already extinct. Wild turkey populations were, like those of the wolf, trumpeter swan, and pronghorn antelope, literally decimated. The fate of the bison was particularly pitiful. It was killed by the millions only for its tongue or hide and was driven almost to extinction in only a decade.

Wild turkey populations survived the carnage only in certain heavily wooded, swampy, and mountainous regions removed from human population centers. Any of these flocks that were commercially hunted, however, also disappeared. Laws to protect the wild turkey and other game from market hunting were much too liberal to be effective. Another problem was that there were no conservation officers; sheriffs and constables had limited enthusiasm for enforcing the new game laws. Furthermore, the laws were not supported by the public and, with virtually no enforcement, were widely ignored.

The wild turkey was particularly vulnerable to market hunting because it was easily baited with grain. Turkeys were killed in large numbers when the flocks came to feed on the bait. Any woodsman could lay his bait in a straight line and kill an entire flock with a single shotgun blast.

Early efforts at wildlife conservation were seen as a way only to delay the extinction of dwindling game supplies and to make sure that the remaining stock was equitably shared even as it was slowly exterminated. There was little thought that wild game could be saved from eventual extinction. Such a naive and erroneous philosophy encouraged the selfish and destructive attitude of "If I don't get it, somebody else will," and excessive hunting continued despite the laws. Wild turkey populations continued to disappear (Table 1).

Even had the game laws of the late 1800s been enforced, this would have done little to bring the turkey

Hunting parties like this one of the 1880's hunted the turkey to extinction in some parts of its range. (Photo courtesy of Kansas State Historical Society, Topeka, Kansas)

back to the large regions of the continent from which it had already been eradicated. Much of the habitat in the East and Midwest had since been clearcut or plowed and would be unsuitable for wild turkeys for many years to come. Restocking was seen as necessary where habitat existed, and was tried sporadically, but the efforts failed because the stock used was semi-domestic and genetically unsuited for life in the wild. Nothing was working for the wild turkey. Much was working against it.

Fortunately for the wild turkey, a better wildlife conservation philosophy was on the horizon. By the end of the 19th century there was a gradual awareness that wildlife did not need to give way entirely to the onslaught of man. Managing game animals as crops was an idea embraced by a few intuitive conservation-minded leaders. The Boone and Crockett Club and similar organizations were formed and successfully sought better conservation laws. Hunting regulations

were given more positive attention than before. A few game wardens were hired in some states and given the specific responsibility of enforcing game laws. Although market hunting was not stopped, it was curtailed to the point that turkey populations were not at the mercy of unregulated hunting.

By the 1930s, many state wildlife agencies were beginning to operate more effectively because of stronger public support and because of the scientific principles employed as part of the new field of wildlife management. The difference between wild and tame turkeys was finally recognized, at least to the more enlightened biologists and naturalists of the day, and the wild turkey was being successfully restored in some parts of its range by trapping and transporting wild turkeys to suitable vacant habitat.

The first wild turkey trap-transplant program took place in New Mexico in 1928 (Ligon, 1946). In the East, a pioneer in the trap-transplant work, and one of the first college-trained American wildlife management biologists to work on the wild turkey, was the late Henry S. Mosby, professor of wildlife management at the Cooperative Fish and Wildlife Research Unit at Virginia Polytechnic Institute. His book, *The Wild Turkey in Virginia*, published in 1943, was the first scientific book to be written about the wild turkey.

Today, wild turkey restoration in the United States has largely been accomplished and is a notable achievement. In 1969, Florida became the first state to complete a statewide restoration program. Missouri completed its program soon afterward, followed by Alabama. Several states now have turkey populations almost everywhere within their boundaries where there is suitable habitat. During the past 45 years, the wild turkey has been reinstated throughout its original range. Wild populations also exist in 11 states outside the wild turkey's ancestral range. The species occurs in 49 of the 50 states of the U.S. and has been successfully introduced into Europe. There are now more than three million turkeys in the U.S. and Mexico, and many U.S. populations are still growing.

Photo courtesy the author.

Following page — Identification band on the leg of a mature gobbler, evidenced by the fully-formed spur. (Photo courtesy the author)

1948

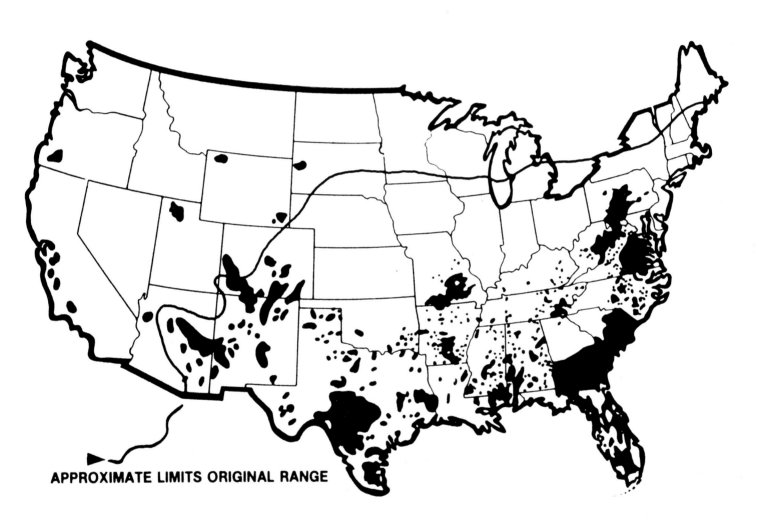

APPROXIMATE LIMITS ORIGINAL RANGE

The range of the wild turkey in the United States at its lowest ebb — 1948. (Based on Walker, E. A. 1949. The Status of the Wild Turkey West of the Mississippi River; and Mosby, H. S. 1949. The Present Status and the Future Outlook of the Eastern and Florida Wild Turkeys in **Transactions North American Wildlife Conference** *14:336-358.)*

1974

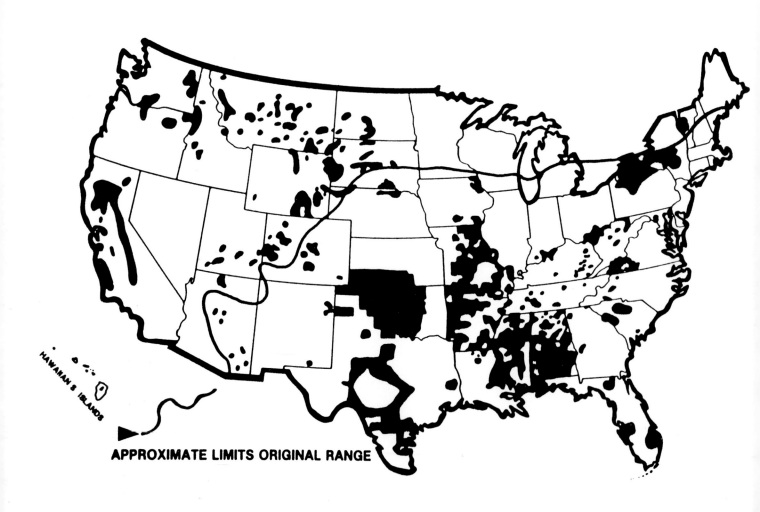

APPROXIMATE LIMITS ORIGINAL RANGE

Range of the turkey re-established through transplants. (Based on Mosby, H. S. 1975. The Status of the Wild Turkey in 1974.)

OBSERVATIONS OF A DYING BREED

Last recorded wild turkey observations prior to reintroduction.

STATE	LOCALITY LAST SEEN	YEAR
Massachusetts	Mount Tom	1851
Connecticut	Totoket Mt., Northford	1813
New York	Allegheny & other countries	1944
Ohio	Wooster & other countries	1878
Michigan	Van Buren County	1897
Indiana	Bickness, Decker Twsp.	1906
Wisconsin	Carlington, Lafayette County	1881
Iowa	Lee County	1907
Nebraska	Ft. Niobrara	1880
Kansas	Ft. Hays	1871
Illinois	Bartelso, Clinton County	1903
South Dakota	Union and Clay Counties	1875

To prepare for cannon netting of turkey specimens, the net has been gathered in a thin line, baited, and the cannons placed and loaded. (Photo courtesy the author)

A flock of turkeys is feeding on the bait line. (Photo courtesy the author)

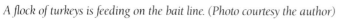

HOW TURKEYS ARE STUDIED

As recently as 1960, little scientific information was available on the wild turkey's behavior, population dynamics, predation, ranging habits, reproduction, or its other vital life processes. Not even the wild turkey's physical features were fully understood. Most of the existing photographs and paintings of the birds were posed for by domestic turkeys or hybrids.

Although some research was done on the turkey's food habits, population status, and basic molting patterns, attempts to study the species alive in its natural habitat were largely unrewarding because it was difficult to study such a scarce and wary animal. The wildlife biologists of the day, who were not very abundant themselves, found easier subjects to study. So, information critical to effective wild turkey management was lacking long after it was badly needed and long after the conservation movement was ready for it.

In the 1950s, advances in electronics technology made it possible to place small radio transmitters on wild animals and track them by radio signals. My colleagues and I, then beginning our studies of the wild turkey, saw the potential in the new radiotelemetry technique. In 1965, we ordered the first transmitters to be used on wild turkeys. The radio-instrumented wild turkeys in our tests could be closely monitored from a distance and found at will. Telemetry was exactly what was needed for studying the elusive wild turkey. Capturing a wild turkey alive to attach a transmitter to it can be the most difficult part of studying wild populations of the birds. Some of the first attempts with turkey traps in the early 1900s were adaptations of wild hog traps made of wooden rails. Grain was placed at the entranceways to entice the birds inside, and tunnels were often dug as entranceways. Regardless of the improvements made, however, walk-in style traps were never very effective for capturing trap-shy wild turkeys.

Better methods employed nets. One netting method is called the "drop-net," a suspended net that falls straight down on a baited turkey flock by the force of gravity. Another method is the "cannon net," which uses explosive charges to propel a net over the flock. The cannon net is especially suited for use with wild turkeys because it can be concealed. By the time the cannons are fired, the net is moving rapidly over the surprised turkeys and it is too late for them to escape. They are, by then, trapped under the descending net.

A trapping method developed during our research employs drugs administered orally through ingested bait (Williams, 1966). When turkeys eat drug-laced baits, they go to sleep and awaken a few hours later in darkened, padded boxes. The birds are later fitted with tiny transmitters and released. Drugged birds experience less trauma than birds that are physically trapped, making them good subjects for behavioral studies.

Turkey transmitters weigh less than 80 grams, or a little less than three ounces, batteries included. This is approximately the weight of a single turkey egg and an insignificant burden for a wild turkey hen. The transmitters emit radio signals for up to a year. The signals identify the birds individually and can be heard over sensitive receivers from a mile away. Some models use solar cells and can transmit for more than a year; others have features that monitor body motion to detect when turkeys are killed by predators or die of other causes.

By using radio-tracking techniques we would be able

The net is fired. (Photo courtesy the author)

The net envelops the flock. (Photo courtesy the author)

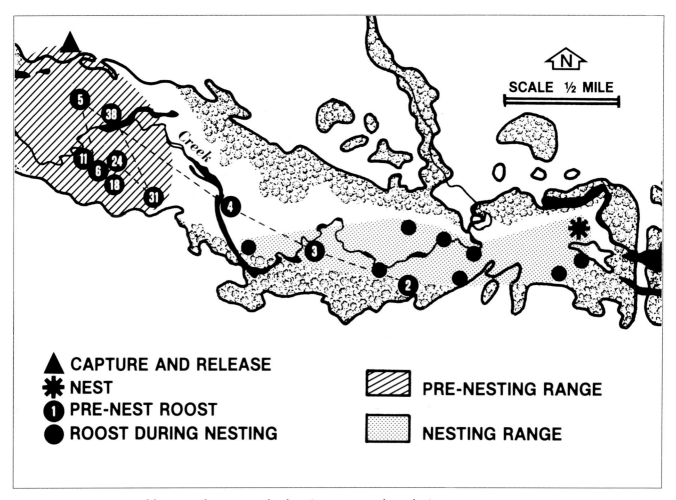

Representative map of the range of a nesting turkey hen. (Map courtesy the author)

to find turkey roosts and determine how to identify and manage roosting habitat. We could locate sick or dead birds and possibly determine the impacts of disease and the causes of death. Daily movement could be mapped to show the turkey's range requirements and habitat preferences. Turkeys being legally and illegally hunted could be monitored to determine harvest patterns and hunting impacts on the populations. Other important biological information obtainable by telemetry included observations on longevity and survival, activity patterns, growth and molting rates, and just about anything else of interest about the birds.

However, it was the possibility of finding turkey nests that most intrigued us. Few wild turkey nests had ever been found by biologists, except by accident, and the

wild turkey's reproductive behavior was an enigmatic aspect of its life history. Nesting ecology was to be our first research focus. Later, we would study the other aspects of the bird's biology.

We radio instrumented 800 wild turkeys during our 14-year project. During the nesting ecology phase of the study, 400 hens were instrumented, enabling us to find 248 wild turkey nests. We discovered when and where the hens nested. From observation blinds we were able to watch the behavior of laying, incubating, and hatching. After hatching, it was possible to track broods and observe their growth, behavior, habitat preferences, and survival. Much of the following account is based on observations made possible by radiotelemetry.

Page 45 — (Gary Griffen photo)

Preceding spread — Turkeys have an established social understanding of each bird's "personal space," which is violated only at the cost of a battle. (Gary Griffen photo)

The confrontation. (Gary Griffen photo)

BEHAVIOR

A zoology professor once said, tongue in cheek: "A wild animal is half anatomy and half behavior." It was a good point, but after working with turkeys for some 30 years, I am inclined to believe wild turkeys are at least three-quarters behavior. A turkey without its unique wild behavior would be no turkey at all.

Mammals have brains designed for learning and storing large amounts of information, and the young of many mammal species learn to survive on their own only through parental care and example. Their useful behavioral patterns, then, develop over long periods. In comparison, birds learn relatively little but are born with an amazing repertoire of instinctive behavior.

I have hatched wild turkey eggs in incubators and observed the poults as their innate patterns of behavior unfolded. They learned to fly on schedule and began roosting in trees the first night out of the pen. They recognized predators and showed instinctive alertness to danger, ducking into cover at the first sight of a hawk soaring overhead. They captured and ate insects without being shown how and preferred the same foods as other wild turkeys. When spring came, they strutted and mated in the normal way. One hen moved more than a mile from my farm to find a mate and returned with a brood of her own in June.

Even the strongest instincts, however, require fine tuning. Wild turkeys will, based on experience, make small adjustments in their behavior. Even so, the turkey is mostly a creature of instinct.

The Social Turkey

The four types of wild turkey flocks are: 1) family flocks, made up of brood hens with their young; 2) adult hen flocks, comprised of hens that were not successful in hatching poults; 3) adult gobbler flocks, comprised of gobblers that regrouped following the mating season, and 4) immature gobbler flocks that form in late fall when the young males leave the family flocks. After the immature gobblers break off from the family flocks, the family flocks contain only hens, both young and adult.

From 30 to 45 percent of the fall turkey population will be young-of-the-year birds. The sex ratio of these young birds is about 50:50. Nearly one-half of the adult hen population will be in family flocks with these poults. The other adult hens are in hen-only flocks without poults. Summer hen-only flocks sometimes number 20 or more birds in good populations.

In early summer, most adult gobblers rejoin the same flocks they were in before the spring flocks broke up. Absent are those that did not survive the mating season. Adult gobbler flocks may contain up to 25 or more birds, but social conditions are unstable in very large flocks, and most adult gobblers form flocks of a dozen or fewer.

There is a tendency for adult gobblers to outnumber adult hens in unhunted populations, probably because the hens are more vulnerable to predation when nesting and accompanying poults. In hunted populations,

Pages 50-51 — Members of an all-jake flock strut and display in the beginning stages of establishing a social hierarchy. (Gary Griffen photo)

Page 52 — Challenge accepted. (Gary Griffen photo)

there are usually more hens because of the selectivity of hunters who prefer to take males and leave the hens.

When the young males outgrow their mothers in the fall, relations between the sexes begin to deteriorate in the family flocks because the brood hens can no longer dominate the jakes. By winter, the young males have separated from the family flocks and formed flocks of their own. Some jakes try to associate with adult gobblers in late winter and spring, but are not welcomed. The all-jake flocks change in size and composition during winter, but by late spring the jakes organize themselves into units with an internal social hierarchy. These flocks will become the larger adult gobbler flocks of the following year when the birds are one and a half years old. At that time the young gobblers will have beards over seven inches long, shiny new plumage, and all the other characteristics of adult gobblers.

Within the flocks, social status is maintained by what is called the "peck order." There is moderate anarchy until the peck order is settled. Rank is achieved by fighting or by using threatening body postures and vocalizations. The top positions are normally occupied by the larger and more-aggressive turkeys. The one at the top has its way with all others in the flock. The bird immediately under it in rank is superior to all except the top bird, and so on down the line. Any time a high-ranking turkey leaves the flock or appears vulnerable due to injury, sickness, or old age, some of the others will fight it, and then each other, to claim its place in the hierarchy.

Turkey fights are started by antagonistic vocal signals and threatening body language. When one turkey walks closely in front of another, it is considered a violation of personal space and a serious affront. When the challenge is intended, the head of the challenger is tilted upward. This is reminiscent of the human "nose in the air" posture of aloofness. Loud *purring* and the antagonistic *whippoorwill* and *threat cooing* calls are issued repeatedly by the challenging turkey. If the challenge is accepted, the calls are answered in kind by the challenged one and the battle begins. Fights are

The fighting begins in earnest. (Gary Griffen photo)

Photo courtesy the author.

Following spread — In the thick of battle. (Gary Griffen photo)

accompanied by thrashing wings and the raucous *fighting rattle* call, which sometimes attracts all turkeys within hearing distance.

If a challenged turkey does not wish to fight, it can turn away quickly and avoid the attention of the challenger. Sometimes the challenged must leave the immediate area to avoid fighting, but simply declining the challenge and acknowledging its subordinate social position usually suffices.

Gobblers begin fighting by striking out with their wings and jumping into the air to use their leg spurs. As fighting progresses, they use their bills to grasp each other by the skin of the head, or by the snood, and tussle to push the opponent backward. The winner normally pursues the loser in a chase through the woods to punctuate his victory. The defeated bird can recognize the superior and will run away at his approach and try to avoid face-to-face contact with him for the remainder of the mating season but may continue to live in the area.

The social hierarchy within the female flocks is established by fighting and threatening as in the male flocks. Hens fight primarily with wings and claws as they bounce into the air and sometimes peck at each other with their bills. I have never seen a hen grasp another by the head as gobblers do.

Fighting is especially frequent early in the mating season when adult gobblers meet for the first time. When small mating alliances fight each other, the entourage with the most gobblers usually wins. In some cases, two immature males can defeat a single adult gobbler if they stand up to him. Immature males also fight for social status within their jake-only flocks.

Besides the fighting that commonly occurs within groups to establish the peck order, and between mating groups in spring, there is also fighting between flocks in fall and winter in which whole groups participate as units. I once saw two flocks of adult gobblers, totaling 48 birds, collide and fight for 20 minutes. Turkeys do not show strong territorial behavior, but the fighting between flocks may suggest at least some sense of territorial affinity.

The final flailing of feathers. (Gary Griffen photo)

Minor injuries from fighting are commonplace. Surface wounds are often visible on the legs and breasts of many adult gobblers. My colleague David Austin once saw a young gobbler killed in a fight, from a blow to its head. An autopsy revealed the cause of death to be a bruise that produced a large blood clot which pressed on the bird's spinal column.

The Turkey's Voice

Vocalizations are vital to the wild turkey. The species has at least 30 distinct calls and is one of the most vocal of birds. The sounds are only signals, however: Turkeys do not construct anything resembling sentences when they communicate. The *gobble*, for instance, is used by the adult male simply to call hens for mating. The *whippoorwill call* warns an adversary to turn away or get read to fight. The *fighting rattle* tells other turkeys in the vicinity that a fight is occurring.

The several alarm calls of the wild turkey illustrate the acoustical features of the sounds. The *alarm putt* is a sharp, loud note made when a stalking predator is spotted while it is too far away to strike. The call is made very loudly to be easily heard by all the birds in the flock as well as by the more distant predator. It is difficult for a predator to determine the direction of origin of the single note of the alarm putt. All the birds in the flock pipe in with the same note as they see the predator. This spreads the risk of exposure throughout the flock but distracts the predator, at least temporarily, from concentrating on an individual turkey.

If a predator surprises a flock, other appropriate calls are used. One, the *predator alarm*, is a harsh sound made as a turkey dodges an attack. It is a sound that is unlikely to be mistaken for any other noise. Since the other birds are close by, it does not need to be very loud, and it isn't. A brood hen sometimes gives the very loud *distress scream* if her young brood is attacked. The call communicates to the poults the extreme danger of the situation. When a poult is captured, it will give its own smaller version of the same distress scream, and some of the other poults may dash for denser cover in a last

Victor and vanquished. (Gary Griffen photo)

resort effort to escape.

When a turkey's suspicions are raised by some object in its immediate vicinity, but no serious alarm is intended, the alert turkey will sound a rapid *alarm pit-pit-pit*. The others will then stand alert to watch. Sometimes others in the flock will also give this call as each spots the suspicious animal. No action will be taken, but all eyes will be open until suspicions are dismissed.

A turkey poult makes its first calls even before it hatches. When the hen hears a poult's *peeping*, she answers with her *hatching yelp*. This communication between hen and hatching brood stimulates the transformation of the hen from a mere feathered incubator into a protective mother. As the poults hatch, the hen can associate their forms with the sounds they make, and the poults can see the source of the comforting calls they heard while still inside the eggshell. The importance of communications between the hen and her poults is paramount. Experiments have shown that if the hen is deafened and cannot hear the poults calling, she will peck them to death as she would so many tiny pests invading the nest.

The poult's peeping and the hen's hatching yelp are soft and difficult to locate. They are not designed to be located, however, nor to be heard any farther than the inches that separate the hen and poults. To make a sound that a predator might key on would be a deadly mistake and one that nature has not favored in the evolution of the wild turkey's voice.

The hen will utter a guttural, segmented call when a large bird flies close over the nest. When this *predator alarm* is given, the newly hatched poults duck under her body and become still and quiet. Another call used by the hen at hatching time is the peculiar *hatching hoot*, which may also be an alarm or scolding note. These commands are obeyed instinctively by the poults, who are still too young and inexperienced to detect many forms of danger on their own.

As it pushes out of the shell and feels the cool air for the first time, or when stepped on by the hen, a poult will give a distress call similar to the distress scream made by older turkeys. The hen will quickly respond by making room under her breast and brooding the poult. This is the same distress call a poult will give if it is caught by a predator.

Even after the last poult has hatched, the brood will spend at least another half day in the nest. If the hen should try to move the brood any sooner, the younger poults would perish because they would not be sufficiently imprinted on the hen to follow her and obey her vocal commands.

When it is time to leave the nest, however, the hen's yelping becomes almost continuous. Then, without hesitation, she rises and moves steadily away from the nest while continuing to call to the brood. The older and better-imprinted poults follow under her feet; the younger linger behind and some may give the three-note *whistled lost call*. The hen will respond to the whistling by stopping to yelp softly, and sometimes by returning part way to the nest to encourage the reluctant poults. All the poults will finally join the hen. She will then turn and resume her course away from the nest, leaving behind a silent cluster of broken eggshells in a shallow depression of dry leaves.

After the poults become imprinted on their mother, they will not mistake her voice for another hen's. The poults will follow the hen even when they cannot see her through dense ground vegetation and will come to her calling in the darkness if they have been attacked by a predator in the night. Biologists have called in and captured lost two-day-old poults by playing a recording of the voice of their mother that had been recorded at the nest a few hours before.

Many broods experience a predator attack soon after leaving the nest. When the hen sees an attacking predator, such as a fox or bobcat, she utters a low-volume alarm call. The poults respond by creeping a

Pages 60-61 — An autumn flock of juvenal males that has separated from the family flocks. (Gary Griffen photo)

Page 62 — These fighting jakes exhibit the thrashing wings and raucous "fighting rattle" call, which signals a battle that will establish social dominance. (Gary Griffen photo)

few feet and then silently freezing in place. Nobody knows exactly what this call sounds like. It is loud enough to be heard only by the huddling poults. I suspect it is one of the alarm calls used in the nest during hatching, probably the predator alarm or hatching hoot.

The *singing alarm* is used when one of the flock spots a high-flying bird of prey. The call, made by poults and adults alike, is brief, with a rapid high-pitched whining and chirping character. It is sometimes quickly repeated. The call is no louder than necessary to be heard by the flock; it is so distinctly different from other calls that it would not likely be confused with any other turkey sound. Obviously, a call that is designed to alert the flock to imminent danger must not be mistaken for another call. When turkeys hear the singing alarm, they all look to the sky. If attacked by a predatory bird, they will dash wildly for the nearest cover.

The *chattering call* is similar to the singing alarm but may have a different function — no one knows for sure. It is mentioned in wild turkey literature, but I have not recorded it.

If a predator attacks a brood, the hen will give a loud distress scream and rush toward the predator with wings drooping and voice at full volume and will sometimes attack the intruder. This display is designed to distract the predator's attention from the poults while they hide. Even powerful predators are reluctant to persist in their stalking while they are under attack. It's a risky tactic, because hens are sometimes killed by the predators they are distracting. Research has shown that the brooding period is the time of the highest death rate for hens.

While danger is present, the hen will continue to give an *alarm putt* about once every second, commanding the poults to remain still and silent. When the hen is ready to assemble the brood, she will give the *assembly yelp* to bring the poults out of hiding. She will usually repeat the call before silently leaving the area with the survivors. The assembly yelp has good acoustical characteristics for the brood to key on, allowing the poults to find the hen quickly. The assembly yelp of

Sibling poults instinctively remain in close physical proximity to one another. (Gary Griffen photo)

each brood hen sounds different from that of other hens. This makes it easy for poults to recognize their own mother's calling, but these calls are still recognizable as yelps and are much like the *lost yelp*, to be discussed shortly.

When attacked, a summer brood will take to the trees, usually within sight of the predator. They gather after the threat has passed by responding to the hen's assembly yelp.

In early summer, when a brood is flushed by a predator, the poults will remain silent for only about a quarter-hour before beginning to sound the three-note, high-pitched, plaintive whistled lost call. Sometimes the call will be a series of four, rather than three, syllables, repeated at brief intervals. One, then another, poult will begin to call until the woods are filled the sounds of whistling. When the hen returns, she will putt sharply for the brood to be silent.

The whistled lost call is not used by the poult to assemble. Its function is to tell the hen that one of its poults is lost. The hen cannot count her poults, and if she does not hear a lost poult whistling, she will leave it.

The need to hear the whistling lost poults, and to be heard by them, explains why the brood hen returns to the point of flush to assemble the brood. The point of flush is the one place most likely to be an equal distance from all the scattered poults.

In mid-summer, the lost whistles of poults are mixed with the broken sounds of changing young voices. What once were the clear, high-pitched notes of the lost whistle are now the *kee-kee*. When the musical notes of the kee-kee are mixed with coarser yelping notes, the call is termed the *kee-kee run*. In late summer, separated poults use the kee-kee and kee-kee-run and will assemble among themselves as they work their way toward the point of flush to join the brood hen.

Young turkeys also use the *plain cluck*, a close-range call used after other calls have brought the turkeys close together but when they still cannot see each other through the vegetation. Adult turkeys will also use the plain cluck under such circumstances.

The plain cluck sounds much like the alarm putt.

Poults that become separated from the hen will sound the three-note, high-pitched, plaintive whistled lost call. (Gary Griffen photo)

Both calls are used to gain the attention of nearby turkeys. The alarm putt is somewhat harsher in tone than the cluck and indicates possible danger for the flock, but an alarm putt does not cause an individual turkey or a flock to leave the scene. A turkey must usually detect danger visually to become that alarmed.

To ensure proper spacing when traveling and feeding, and to do this without having to watch each other constantly, a turkey flock makes *purring* sounds almost continuously while on the move. This reserves a small, exclusive space around each bird and keeps the flock together. Purring can be very soft or extremely loud. Soft purring cannot be heard beyond a short distance but is probably easy to track at very close range. Soft purring signals harmony and well-being in the flock. Loud purring indicates irritation. Between the extremes of soft and loud purring, the flock's level of irritation is matched by the harshness of the turkeys' purring.

Two calls used by turkeys to threaten each other are the *threat call* and *threat coo*. Both are heard when one turkey walks closely in front of another, thereby violating its personal space. Unless the offending bird moves out of the way, purring becomes louder and escalates into the loud *fighting rattle*. The threatening postures and body movement that accompany the fighting rattle signal the beginning of a turkey fight.

As fighting proceeds, the volume and intensity of rattling continues. The slamming of wings and loud rattling make a noise that few turkeys within hearing range can ignore. Fighting may draw a crowd. The noise is probably intended to draw attention so other turkeys will notice significant changes in the social order. Sometimes whole flocks fight each other as units, thereby forming dominance relationships between flocks.

The vocabulary of young turkeys in family flocks changes little from late summer to fall except for the gradual lowering of voice pitch as the young birds grow larger. During the summer, however, the poults do begin to use the plain yelp, lost yelp, and tree yelp.

The *plain yelp* is a multi-purpose call of from three to eight notes, and great variation is heard from one rendition to another, even when given by the same bird. It probably has several functions, depending on context, including identification of the caller as a turkey as well as indicating the direction of the caller. This is the same call that is sometimes referred to as the "love call" of the hen. It changes into the lost yelp in its louder and longer versions.

The *lost yelp* is used mainly by adults and sometimes by older juveniles when members of the flock are separated. The call has good acoustical characteristics for determining course directions. It is loud enough to be heard over considerable distances.

The *tree yelp* is emitted upon awakening on the roost in the morning and appears to be an "all is well" signal as well as an inquiry asking "Is everybody still here?" It has a soft, nasal quality and cannot be heard beyond the roost area. It is too soft to be useful for long-distance calling.

The members of a flock sometimes give a *feeding call* when they bunch closely together at a good patch of food, but this call cannot be heard beyond the diameter of the flock and does not call other turkeys to feed. It is a combination of soft putting and purring and is probably a spacing call that signals mild irritation over the closeness of feeding flockmates.

Roost pitting is a distinctive, high-pitched clucking call made by a mildly disturbed flock on the roost. It is not loud. The turkeys in the roosting flock give "pitts" at irregular intervals, making it difficult for a man, or predator, to key on any one bird from the direction of the sound. I believe the call's function is to confuse predators spotted in the roosting area.

When a flock of young turkeys is scattered and some are calling, one that discerns danger may give the *hush*

Preceding spread — The bobcat is one of the major predators of adult wild turkeys. (Photo courtesy the author)

This hen is issuing the assembly yelp call to bring her poults out of hiding following the passing of the threat of danger. Her assembly yelp sounds different from that of any other hen, assuring that her poults will recognize it as that of their mother. (Gary Griffen photo)

call to silence the others. This call is a series of about five to eight brief chirps in rising pitch.

When a flock has been hunted heavily, separated turkeys are reluctant to yelp loudly. They may use only the *single yelp* or *double yelp* when searching for their flockmates as they return to the place they were scattered. These notes may merely be abbreviated lost yelping. More study is needed to determine that with certainty.

Young turkeys in winter flocks are more self-reliant and, when separated, are not "lost" to the degree a dependent poult may be when away from its mother and flockmates. *Loud clucking*, also termed "cutting," is heard when a yelping turkey is being answered from a distance by another turkey that is not lost. The way it is used suggests that it tells the lost bird that if the two are to get together, the lost bird will have to do the walking. A turkey looking for its flock will also use loud clucking while conducting its search.

The *whit-whit* is used along with loud clucking and in much the same way. Both loud clucking and the whit-whit are used by turkeys as early as their first winter of life.

The *cackle*, also termed "flying cackle," is used only when turkeys fly, but not every time they do so. Some versions of the cackle are as brief as one note, but an elaborate, full cackle may have more than 20 notes.

Calls made exclusively by the male are the *gobble*, to call hens for mating, and the *chump* and *hum*, the two sounds associated with strutting. The chump sound is sometimes called "spitting," but that is misleading because saliva is not involved.

Some males can gobble when only a few months old, and many jakes gobble in spring, as do the adult gobblers. Jake gobblers can strut, and even hens will strut occasionally, but I have never heard a hen gobble and I don't know whether strutting hens make the chump and hum sounds of the strutting gobbler.

The calls of young male and female turkey poults are indistinguishable. The differences in the tonal qualities of adult hens and gobblers are sometimes difficult to distinguish — their voices overlap in pitch. This is revealed by voice diagrams made from recordings. Both hens and gobblers have a raspy voice quality when yelping loudly. The voice simply "breaks," as yours may if you holler loudly. The main distinction between the voices of the hens and of the gobblers is that the voice of the grown male turkey, the older jake included, has a bugling or reverberant quality due to the male's larger throat.

The wild turkey probably has more than 31 calls. I have heard several that I have not discussed here because I have not recorded them and do not know enough about them. It is possible that a few of those listed will eventually be found to be only variations of the other calls. The exact number of calls and their meanings will not be known until more research is done on the turkey's voice and vocabulary. Even then there will be room for differing interpretations and differences of opinion among those who have studied the subject.

Wild turkey vocalizations have not gone unnoticed by mankind. Imitated calling has been the major strategy used in hunting the wild turkey since Native American times, and scores of different types of calling instruments are used by hunters today. Perhaps the oldest is the classic wingbone yelper made from the cleaned and polished bones of the wild turkey itself.

In addition to its voice, the wild turkey also uses body language to convey messages at close range. The changing colors of the gobbler's head is an example. The threatening spread wings and tail posture that precede fighting is a warning for an adversary to back down or prepare to fight. The head-up posture of superiority is another example. The posture of the strutting gobbler is body language advertising his mating intentions, and the squatting of a receptive hen before a strutting gobbler tells the gobbler that his advances have been accepted.

An Intelligent and Wary Bird

The wild turkey is famous for its wariness. Taking a wild turkey is no easy feat for human hunter or animal

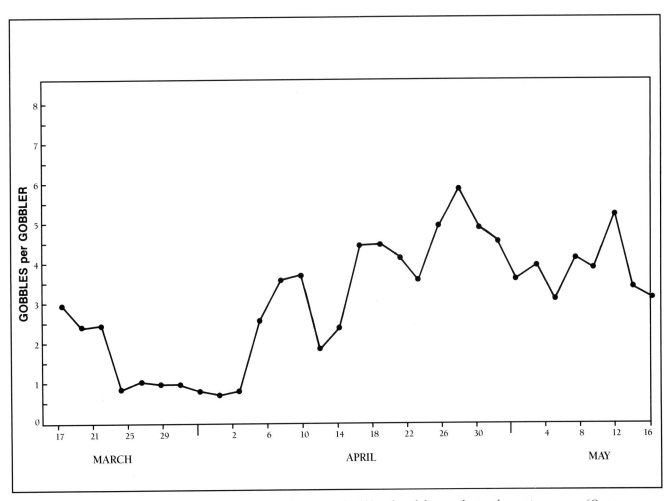

A sample graph showing the typical pattern in the frequency of gobbling by adult toms during the mating season. (Courtesy the author)

predator. The turkey's keen senses, constant alertness, and uncompromising sense of caution are inherited as part of its genetic code. With predation a daily threat from egg to adult, there is little time for a wild turkey to learn from experience.

Innate defensive behavior is especially crucial to the survival of vulnerable young broods. A hen with a young brood watches any approaching animal closely. If the animal acts like a predator as it approaches, the hen will crouch and quietly order the poults to hide. She will not move or twitch even if the predator approaches within a few feet. Staying still in the presence of a predator is a hazardous tactic but one that is clearly in the best interest of the brood. If the predator has not seen the hen, it will pass, and the brood will be safe and will soon resume its activities.

But sometimes the predator spots the brood hen. By paying close attention, the hen is able to know the instant the predator spots her and will order the poults to remain hidden as she springs up to feign a broken wing or to attack the predator to divert its attention from the brood. The ploy often works — even a strong predator is reluctant to continue stalking when it is under attack itself. Often, the poults hide so effectively that the predator is unaware of their presence. If the hen is successful with this ruse, the predator will follow the hen away from the spot or stop stalking due to the hen's harassment.

Such behavior makes the hen almost as vulnerable as the brood. If the hen exercised her ability to escape from the predator, she would effectively sacrifice the brood as they would be defenseless without her. Hens without broods take no such chances; they evade predators at much greater distances and, if approached closely, will fly or run away to save themselves, leaving nothing behind but their tracks and a disappointed predator.

The reason broodless hens flock separately from

71

hens with broods is to avoid the dangers of being with poults. Conversely, the reason broods flock separately from broodless turkeys is to avoid dangers that would befall the brood by being with turkeys that have only their own self interests to protect.

A wild turkey recognizes a predator by its behavior. It does not have to acquire, through natural selection or long personal experience, a visual image of every type of predator it may encounter. A predator in any disguise will still behave as a predator. The reason that man is feared by many species of animal, even some that never saw a man, is because animals recognize the predator-like behavior of humans. Our binocular vision, combined with the intent interest we exhibit toward wild animals, reveals us as the predatory species we have always been.

Wild turkeys are also instinctively cautious of certain types of animals, regardless of their behavior. A snake at close range will sometimes send a turkey into near hysteria, whether it has ever had personal experience with a snake or not. A hawk flying overhead is recognized immediately as a danger, even by poults that never saw a hawk before. These are universal predator forms to which many prey species have evolved instinctive avoidance reactions.

Wild turkeys may become less wary of man if exposed to people without being molested, but that takes much time during which trust must gradually be established and scrupulously maintained. I once watched a ranch manager feed wild turkeys in a remote part of the ranch by rattling shelled corn in a metal coffee can as he had done at the same time of morning for more than three years. The rattling sound quickly called in 50 wild turkeys, some to within 10 feet of him. I had to remain hidden to see this demonstration because the turkeys trusted only him, not humans in general.

Wild turkeys can be fully tamed only by "parental imprinting" on humans. Hatchling wild turkeys in-stinctively associate themselves with the first large moving object they see at the time of hatching, as previously discussed. Under normal circumstances, that would be their mother. However, if turkey eggs are hatched in an artificial incubator and a person broods and talks to them during the first three days of life, the poults will imprint mentally on the person and the young birds will have no fear of humans. The tame behavior is permanent and is exhibited toward all humans, not only the individual that acted as parent. That is probably the way the wild turkey was domesticated by Indians in Mexico two thousand years ago.

Usually, though, wild turkeys avoid humans, as they do natural predators. Normal behavior for an adult wild turkey that is startled at close range by a human is to fly about 250 yards, land in a tree, and remain there for about one hour. If not further disturbed, it will fly to the ground and resume its routine activities. Nothing in the turkey's evolutionary history has required it to move more than a few yards to avoid an enemy. A human is perceived as another predator to be evaded but one that will likely show up again at another time and place, and not one that can be permanently eluded by moving to a new home range.

Movement Behavior

An animal needs to know where to find its food, water, cover, and other requirements for living. When these resources are found, wild animals do not roam aimlessly around. The area a turkey uses regularly and in which it finds the necessities for life is called its *home range*.

The wild turkey and most other animals also have a *minimum cruising range* that they will traverse, even though they may not need to travel that far to feed or obtain other daily requirements. The minimum cruising range of wild turkeys has not been accurately

Preceding spread — A tom in fully displayed mating plumage struts, chumps and hums to gain the attention of a potential mate. Note the large breast sponge. (Gary Griffen photo)

Photo courtesy the author.

Following spread — *The body language of two strutting gobblers indicates that mating season is in full swing. (Gary Griffen photo)*

measured. I would estimate it to be around 100 to 200 acres for fall flocks of wild turkeys, at least where I have studied them intensively in Florida. How much larger the home range is than the minimum cruising range depends on the quality of the habitat — the better the habitat, the smaller the area required to support a turkey and the less one tends to travel. This somewhat oversimplifies the relationship between habitat quality and movement, but the relationship is a very close one.

Home ranges are measured by connecting points of travel on a map. The home range area is enclosed within the outer points of travel. Movement over several days is observed and averaged to calculate a daily home range.

An incubating hen has the smallest daily home range of any turkey, spending more than 90 percent of her time on one square foot of ground that is her nest and seldom using an area of more than 20 acres when she is on recess. After the brood hatches, a summer family flock in good habitat will have a daily home range of 300 to 400 acres, conforming to topographic, vegetative, and man-made features of the landscape.

Fall and winter daily home ranges of family flocks may be as small as 200 to 400 acres for extended periods in excellent habitat or as large as 2,000 acres in poor habitat. Turkeys do not occur where the habitat is so poor that they cannot move somewhere within it to find the resources they need.

A flock uses the same home range as long as the resources within it fulfill the flock's requirements, but the boundary is ill-defined and constantly changing as food supplies and other resources are exhausted or changes occur within the seasons. Large shifts in home range occur in the fall and spring when environmental conditions and social relationships change most rapidly. As range shifts occur over time, the area utilized increases when viewed in retrospect. This cumulative effect results in an "annual" home range much larger than the daily, weekly, monthly, or seasonal range of the flock or individual bird.

I do not believe a "lifetime home range" has ever been measured for a wild turkey. The exact size of such an area would depend, of course, on how long the turkey lived. We know that when all requirements for living are close at hand, turkeys die within four or five miles of where they hatched. There are always exceptions — movement of 20 miles or more in a lifetime occurs in Texas. However, on better Texas range, turkeys move no farther than they do in other good range.

Merriams turkeys undertake regular migratory movements in their mountainous habitat, to higher elevations in summer and back down to lower elevations in fall. They may move considerable distances in the process. Little is known about movement of the Goulds turkey, but it is also a mountain bird and its movement behavior is probably similar to the Merriams.

Turkeys have no "homing" instinct. If captured and transported outside their area of familiarity, they will simply establish a new home range at the new site. This behavior has aided turkey restoration programs by minimizing dispersal. Many wild animals — deer, wild boar, bear, and many birds, for example — will try to return home when transported and may move 100 or more miles in the process, completely leaving the area they were intended to restock.

Following page — Photo courtesy the author.

Following page — Photo courtesy the author.

Following page — *Wild turkeys have a minimum cruising range that they will traverse. (Gary Griffen photo)*

Although they are not as heavily feathered as the toms, female turkeys also need to dust occasionally to remove parasites. (Gary Griffen photo)

Preceding page — *Photo courtesy the author.*

CHARACTERISTICS OF THE TURKEY'S VOICE

Descriptions of some of the wild turkey's 31 known calls*

Name Of Call/ Lenght of Notes (In Seconds)	Unusual Number Of Notes	Peculiar Quality, If Any	Beat/ Rhythm	Notes Per Second
Lost Whistling 0.20	3-4	Musical	Waltz-like	4/1.6 sec.
Kee-Kee 0.10-0.15	3	Musical	Uneven	3/1.2 sec.
Kee-kee-run 0.05-0.10	4-10	Variable	Uneven	6/1.8 sec.
Tree yelp (hen) 0.08	3-5	Nasal	Even	6-7
Plain yelp (hen) 0.08-0.10	4-7+	—	Even	6-7
Lost yelp (hen) 0.10-0.15	8-20+	Raspy	Even	6-7
Assembly yelp 0.12-0.20	6-10+	Variable	Even	Variable
Plain cluck 0.04	1-3	Staccato	Uneven	1
Loud clucking 0.04	4-10+	Staccato	Uneven	3-7
Alarm putt 0.04	1+	Staccato	Uneven	1
Cackle Variable	10-15	Excited	Uneven	5

From Williams (1989)

83

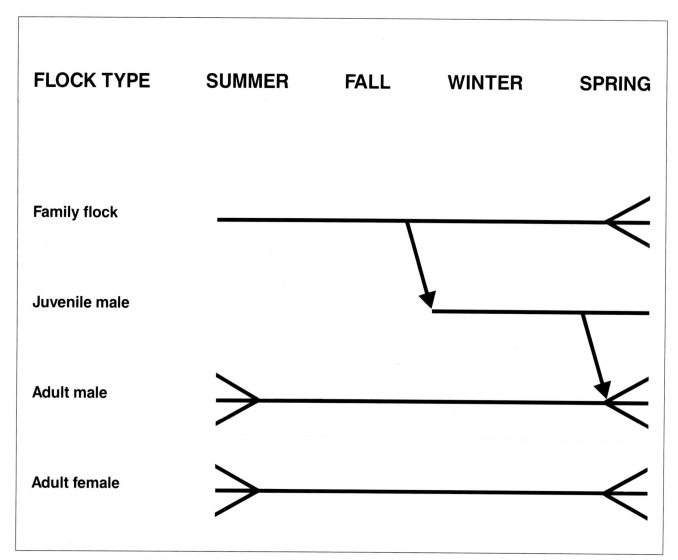

FLOCK TYPE	SUMMER	FALL	WINTER	SPRING

Family flock

Juvenile male

Adult male

Adult female

Diagram of flocking behavior. Read from left to right. Family flocks remain intact until the males leave to form juvenile male flocks in late fall. In spring, juvenile males join adult male flocks. Adult male flocks form in summer and continue intact until spring break up. Hens that were unsuccessful in nesting remain in adult female flocks from spring through winter.

The sign is. . .	Indicates. . .
Many shed feathers	Probable regular roost
Food particles in droppings	Identity of foods eaten
Many tracks in trail	Major travel way
Only old sign (feathers, no tracks)	Turkeys may have shifted range
Old and fresh tracks mixed	Regularly used area
Wing-tip scrapes in soil	Strutting activity

Examples of information indicated by turkey field sign.

THE SEASONAL TURKEY

If a turkey population is to renew itself, many new broods must hatch and enough poults must survive the summer to replace the mortality that occurred during the previous year. That is no small order. About 30 to 40 percent of the turkeys in a population can be expected to die each year of natural causes, and it is a rare turkey that lives to be more than six years old. The oldest known wild turkey was only 12.

The brood is the social unit of the new wild turkey generation. Usually two or more broods join to form a larger summer flock. There are obvious advantages to living among other turkeys — the more eyes and ears in the group, the more likely one is to spot a predator or find food.

Summer family flocks range in size up to 30 or more birds. The members have strong social bonds and know one another. Even stronger ties are evident within each brood. Gobblers, last year's jakes, and hens that were unsuccessful in nesting keep their distance from the family flocks.

One June morning while radio-tracking a family flock comprised of three broods of from five to seven weeks of age, 40 minutes before sunrise I slipped in under the roost and against the sky light could see several of the poults restlessly moving about. One "putted" at me — it had heard my approach. After I was still and well hidden, the poult showed no further concern, but it and several others continued to move about on the tree's limbs. The only adult hen in view was still asleep. The broods were spaced from 30 to 80 feet apart on the lower limbs of cypress trees about 30 feet above the water of a slough.

A few minutes before sunrise, one hen glided silently to the ground, landing about 400 feet from the tree she had slept in, and was followed at five-second intervals by four poults from the same tree. Eight minutes later, a second hen glided down in the same direction as the first and was followed immediately by eight poults. The third brood hen flew down two minutes later, followed by three poults. None of the turkeys had made a sound since the poult had putted at me 30 minutes earlier.

Three minutes later a hen on the ground yelped. The last of the roosting poults flew toward her from the trees. That emptied the roost. One of the three poults glided gracefully into the water of the slough, apparently mistaking it for dry land, and flopped its way to the bank to join the others. A few minutes later, as the first direct sunlight touched the ground outside the swamp, I could see the hens and poults feeding in a grassy glade as they moved out of sight to the north.

Summer family flocks are sometimes accompanied by broodless hens. I believe these hens join a flock when they have poults of their own and remain with the family flock after their poults are lost to predation.

In summer the hens are recovering from the rigors of nesting and they, as well as turkeys of all ages, are molting heavily. At one stage, young turkeys are simultaneously carrying remnants of three different plumage generations, and nearly one-third of the new feathers of the adult are growing in at the same time.

Following page — Just after sunrise, a hen glides silently from the night's roost to the ground. Her poults will soon follow her example and join her. (Marcia Griffen photo)

As they mature, young birds of most species have three successive plumages. First, natal down; second, the juvenal plumage, and finally the first winter plumage. But the young wild turkey has an extra plumage between the juvenal and first winter plumage that is necessitated by an extremely rapid growth rate which literally causes the bird to outgrow its feathers. After they mature, however, turkeys molt only once each year.

Even under threat of death in the talons of a predator, the wild turkey's daily routines must proceed, and the nutritional requirements of body growth and molting must be met by heavy feeding on nutritious summer foods. Fortunately, summer days are longer than is usually required for turkeys to feed. When their appetites are satiated after the morning foraging period, turkeys dig shallow scrapes in the cool soil of a shaded place and wallow there to escape the summer heat. Their feathers molting daily, the turkeys constantly preen their plumage to care for tender pin feathers and to oil the new ones. Shed feathers can usually be found in the turkeys' summer wallows. We call this behavior *nooning*.

In summer, turkeys frequently fly into trees and may remain there for an hour or longer, preening and resting. Based on my field observations, I suspect they do this to avoid predators while resting.

No brood goes the summer without a predator attack. When ambushed by a bobcat or fox, the half-grown turkeys will flush wildly into nearby trees and watch the predator. When the danger passes, the flock will assemble at the call of the hen and then calmly go about its regular business. With a little good luck, an alert brood will survive the summer untouched by predators but a little wiser from many close encounters.

Broods feed and rest intermittently during the day and usually have a relatively long rest period around noon. After "nooning" at mid-day, the flock resumes its feeding activities and usually has a mid-afternoon period of especially heavily feeding. Near sundown the flock heads for roosting cover and flies into the trees for the night as the sun sets. Some of the birds will change limbs several times before finding a suitable one for the night.

Sometimes summer broods roost in the same favorite places for extended periods, creating a buildup of shed feathers and droppings on the ground beneath. Heavy stands of medium-sized trees are preferred for roosting, but wild turkeys can be very unpredictable about where they roost. We do know that they rarely sleep in dead trees if living trees are available.

Very young broods sleep close beside the hen, under her outstretched wings. At three or four weeks of age, however, the brood begins to spread out into other trees near the hen and no longer seeks her shelter.

Turkeys of all ages squat on their chosen limb and sleep with their head drawn in on their shoulders or laid under the feathers on top of their wings or back. Some people believe that turkeys stick their heads under their wings to sleep, but I have not observed that behavior and suspect that the belief is due to the misleading appearance of the turkey's head when it is covered by the feathers of the shoulders.

Turkeys in Fall and Winter

As summer days shorten and the year turns toward fall, the trees are beginning to drop their seeds, grasses are laden with seed, and insects are at maximum abundance — there is plenty for wild turkeys to eat. The poults have survived the most critical period of life and have outgrown many of the predators that would take a smaller bird, and the experienced young turkeys have better learned how to elude the rest.

By fall, the young males are larger than their mothers and sisters. They have grown tiny beards on their upper breasts since September and have noticeable bumps for spurs on their lower legs. The fall jake is the epitome of adolescent gangliness and is still growing rapidly.

Young turkeys spend much of the early fall days at play. They chase one another through the woods in a game resembling tag. They will fly at each other, sometimes only barely avoiding collisions. Young males begin to strut like adults, even though they have never seen this behavior before, and the young mock

New poults, unable to fly, must roost in weedy groundcover under the protection of the body and outstretched tail and wings of the hen. (Gary Griffen photo)

many other activities of older birds, including fighting and mating. They also spend much time wallowing, preening, sunning, and dusting.

With leaves falling every day, some of the food becomes covered and has to be scratched out of the leaves. Turkeys have a fixed four-stroke method of scratching. One foot is extended forward and raked back, then the other foot is placed forward and raked back twice. The first foot is again placed forward and raked back once more. This creates a definite and easily recognized four-scratch rhythm: scratch, scratch-scratch, scratch. Most turkeys begin with the right foot although left-footed turkeys are not rare.

By the time winter comes, young turkeys are through molting and resemble adults in appearance. The jakes' beards, which by now barely poke through their breast feathers, distinguish the young males from the older gobblers with their longer beards. Hens, however, do not normally have beards, so young hens look much

like adult hens. There are plumage features that distinguish young hens from old hens in winter, however.

The last juvenal feather in the wing of the young turkey of both sexes is usually retained during the first winter of life and, with its characteristically pointed tip and dull markings, distinguishes juvenal specimens. But this is not useful at a distance. A better way to tell adult hens from the younger females is by the configuration of the "speculum" on the side of the wing.

Winter is a time of heavy feeding and waiting for wild turkeys. All are gaining weight rapidly to fuel their 103-degree body temperature through the cold weather of winter. The adults are building their fat reserves. There is little else for a wild turkey to do now besides eat and avoid being eaten. By winter's end, the turkeys will be at maximum annual weight and ready for the stresses of the mating and brood-rearing season.

Photo courtesy the author.

At least one juvenal outer primary wing feather (far left) is normally retained in the first winter plumage. Its unique, pointed and brownish tip distinguishes yearlings from adults. (Photo courtesy the author)

THE LIFE CYCLE

The Mating Season

Early one warmer-than-usual pre-spring morning, about the time long-dormant redbud trees begin to show the first signs of new life, the gobbles of wild turkeys echo through the swamps and down the valleys. At first, gobbling is sporadic, occurring while the adult males are still in their winter flocks. As the weather warms, though, it brings the adult males into mating condition and gobbling is soon heard throughout the woods.

In early spring, aggressive male tempers flare easily, and fighting occurs as the gobblers try to better their social positions in the flock. This aggressiveness between males results in the large winter flocks breaking into smaller, more-compatible units well in advance of the mating season.

Many gobblers spend the spring alone, gobbling to attract mates; others are content to associate with a more-dominant gobbler and to gobble with him and act as his bodyguard. Sometimes as many as three or four gobblers form a small spring mating alliance, but only the most dominant gobbler in the group will do the mating. Some biologists think these groups are brothers or closely related cousins.

The turkey is polygynous, which means that a gobbler mates with as many hens as he can. He takes no part in nesting or rearing the young. This would not be possible because he may have several mates during the season that go their separate ways. Besides, young turkeys find their own food and need only a single parent to lead them around.

The wild turkey is not strictly territorial. Instead of guarding a geographical mating territory as some animals do, the wild turkey gobbler puts his energy into frequent loud gobbling to attract hens, and tries to accompany all the hens he can throughout the day so he will be on hand when one decides to mate.

Most gobbling occurs at dawn from the turkey's roosting place in a tree. Sound carries farther from the elevated position when the air is still and cool in early morning. Early morning gobbling can sometimes be heard by human ears a mile or more away. Gobblers sometimes also strut and drum while on their roosting limbs.

Gobbling is a long-distance call that tells hens where a gobbler is. The familiar strutting behavior of the male, with puffed out feathers and roundly spread tail, is normally reserved for close-range courting when a hen is present or to show off to other gobblers. Strutting advertises that the dominant gobbler in the entourage is ready to mate, and it may have a facilitating effect on the sexual receptivity of the hen as well.

A strutting gobbler will walk with his feathers puffed and tail partly spread. When a hen is watching him, however, he prefers to move in short semi-circles with his tail spread in a wide circle and his wings scraping the ground. As he struts, the gobbler produces a short "chump" sound from his throat, followed by a low-pitched "drumming" sound that resembles in tone a lower string of a bass violin. In a gobbler mating entourage, all the males sometimes strut and drum simultaneously.

Although it is not very loud, the low pitch of the

Following page — *Most gobbling occurs around dawn from the turkey's roosting place in a tree. The elevated position and cool, still morning air allow the sound to carry farther. (Gary Griffen photo)*

2"

Adult males will gobble to attract females for mating. Some are content to associate with a more dominant gobbler, to gobble with him and act as his bodyguard. Only the more dominant tom will do the mating, however. (Gary Griffen photo)

drumming sound is not easily deflected or absorbed by vegetation. A human with good hearing can hear it from 150 yards on a cool, still morning. No one knows how far a hen can hear it.

Competition for mating privileges leaves a breeding gobbler little time to feed. He must follow the hens and concentrate on gobbling and strutting or risk some other gobbler moving in on the hens he has been courting. Nature has taken care of the conflicting priorities of feeding versus mating by providing the mature male with a large reserve of fat called the "breast sponge." This fat reserve is gained by heavy feeding in fall, winter, and early spring. Large breast sponges can weigh as much as three pounds.

Although most fowl have large fat reserves to help them through the spring breeding season, the fat in the turkey gobbler's breast sponge is especially easy to metabolize. This fat supplies ample body energy while the gobbler forgoes feeding for long periods to focus

his attention on courtship and mating. I do not know of any other bird with a breast sponge quite like a turkey gobbler's. The turkey hen is also very fat in spring but does not have a breast sponge.

As the weather continues to warm in spring, an increasing number of adult gobblers take up gobbling, and hens begin to associate with gobblers more and more. As this new interest in the opposite sex builds, hens exhibit less interest in their own gender, and their winter hen-only flocks begin to dissolve.

The mating urge of the hen is controlled by increasing day-length in spring. Therefore, mating closely correlates with the same calendar dates each year. Although the warmth of spring also plays a role in stimulating mating behavior in the hen, as it does in the gobbler, day-length is probably more important to the hen. There is a good reason for that.

Early season gobbling is not taxing on the males. If the weather turns cold again, they can simply stop

gobbling until warm weather returns. By gobbling and strutting in advance of the mating season, the adult males are attending to the preliminaries of flock dispersal and a new social order. They will be ready to mate before the hens are, and at no great expense. But the hen's commitment to the reproductive process is more binding. She must not be fooled by the weather to mate and nest too early. If she does, she will bring off her poults before true spring arrives, and there will be no insects or succulent green vegetation for them to eat. That would spell disaster for her brood. If all the hens did likewise, it could be catastrophic for the population.

As the days lengthen and the hens begin associating closely with adult gobblers, their presence causes the gobblers to strut more than they gobble, which has the effect of diminishing the overall level of gobbling in the population. Gobbling is not completely terminated, however, because not all the males are accompanied continuously by hens, and even when hens are present, a gobbler will still occasionally gobble.

When a hen is ready to mate, she moves close to the strutting gobbler and squats on the ground. While still in strutting posture, the gobbler approaches from behind, walks slowly up her back, and "treads" as though marching slowly in place. After one to four minutes of treading, the gobbler drops his tail and squats toward the hen and completes the act of copulation.

The time-consuming courtship processes of the wild turkey — and many other species of birds, for that matter — is a kind of "foreplay" made necessary by the fact that the male must place his cloaca in direct contact with the hen's at the very instant she is ready to receive semen. Proper timing is essential. Only through a long pre-copulatory ceremony, "treading" in the wild turkey, can necessary synchrony be achieved.

As the gobbler steps down after copulating, the hen stands and moves away, ruffles her feathers, and usually leaves the immediate area. The gobbler resumes

Photo courtesy the author.

Preceding page — (Gary Griffen photo)

Following page — Gobblers may also strut and drum while on their roosting places. (Gary Griffen photo)

95

Having noticed the strutting tom, the hen moves closer to him and prepares to squat for the tom's "tread." (Gary Griffen photo)

strutting, and, if no hens are in sight, he usually resumes gobbling.

It is not known how many times hens mate in a season or whether they seek the same gobbler when they do. It is known that the domestic turkey hen can continue to lay fertile eggs for several weeks after a single copulation. I suspect a wild hen can do at least as well. Semen is stored in a special vesicle inside the hen and the sperm in it fertilizes each of the eggs as they descend the oviduct, before the albumen or eggshell are added.

Most juvenal males are not sexually mature in their first spring and do not mate. A few can gobble and mate as well as any adult and will show more than casual interest in hens when adult gobblers are not present. Some of these jakes will attempt to associate with the small mating season alliances of adult gobblers, but are usually not welcome. Most immature males form loosely organized flocks of their own and spend the spring on the fringes of the turkey world. These jake-

only flocks are usually the largest flocks in the spring population.

Unlike the young males, who are left out of mating, young hens mate and nest and contribute substantially to the productivity of the population in some years.

The Nesting Hen

After she has mated, the hen becomes a nearly solitary creature. She will move away from her winter haunts and long-time companions to find an old field, grassy fencerow, tangle of vines, or other cover in which to nest.

There is no completely predictable pattern to hen movement at nesting time. Many will occupy habitat they would shun at other seasons and will travel more than a mile to establish a new home range. Some will occupy their nesting range for three to four weeks before beginning to lay, while others will nest soon after

The copulatory tread and mount. (Gary Griffen photo)

moving from their winter range. A few will nest in the same area in which they spent the winter. Hens freely move into range recently deserted by other hens, and many pass each other in the woods as they select their own home ranges for nesting. All of these modes are observed even within the same population, which underscores the extreme variability in the behavior of wild turkeys.

When the hen finds a place to her liking, she does not build a nest in advance of laying, as do most birds. She merely scratches a bare place on the ground and lays the first egg there, usually at mid-day. The hen stands to lay and gently squats as she deposits an egg. Of thousands of wild turkey eggs I have examined, only one was slightly cracked from being dropped too hard on top of another egg.

The hen remains at the nest a few minutes after laying and covers the brown-speckled egg with a few dried leaves picked up from beside the nest. When she leaves

after laying, she might move as far as half a mile to feed.

Most hens skip laying the day after the first egg is deposited and come to lay the second egg on the third day. They again cover their eggs with a few leaves before leaving. Another day is usually skipped, but after laying the third egg, most hens lay an egg per day until their clutch is complete. Each time they lay, they cover their eggs. In that way, nesting material collects as a result of egg-covering and not by intentional nest-building.

When hens come to lay each of their first five eggs, they sit on the nest for an average of about one hour per laying session. When they return to lay the sixth egg, they remain nearly two hours, on average, remain about three hours in laying the seventh egg, and another hour longer on the eighth and each egg after that. By the time the last egg is laid, most hens are coming to their nests around noon and spending the entire afternoon sitting. Incubation thus begins gradually after the fifth egg is laid, and a significant part of the total

A few minutes after laying, the hen covers her brown-speckled eggs with dried leaves picked up from around the nest. (Gary Griffen photo)

incubating requirement has been accomplished before the hen begins sitting on the eggs overnight.

As the hen sits on her partial clutch during the laying period, the feel and sight of the eggs affect her nervous system and initiate hormone secretions that gradually bring on incubation behavior. The hormone, prolactin, also shuts down egg formation in the hen's body as its level in the blood stream increases during late stages of the laying cycle. In more than 200 nests I have observed only one incubated nest contained fewer than five eggs, which suggests that about five eggs are needed to stimulate the prolactin production that shuts down the laying process and starts the gradual onset of incubation behavior. It is an interesting process that deserves further study and is probably not peculiar to the wild turkey.

Hens usually lay from 8 to about 13 eggs per clutch. Most nests contain from 9 to 11 eggs. The average clutch size in the Florida studies was 10.3—adults averaged 10.5

eggs per clutch; juveniles averaged 10.0. The largest clutches of individual hens held 17 eggs. Although two hens sometimes lay in the same nest, multiple clutches will probably not hatch successfully because of the improbability of the two hens coordinating their incubation behavior.

After laying the final egg, hens begin incubating continuously, day and night. During the incubation period, they frequently stir and rearrange the eggs by rolling them with their beaks and spend much time standing over the nest. They leave the nest to take brief recesses about every two days, on average. Hens do not cover their eggs when on recess during the period of continuous incubation behavior as they did while laying.

A hen on recess from incubation duty moves about hurriedly as she feeds on green vegetation, perhaps gets a drink of water, and defecates. She takes different routes when returning to the nest, which makes it very difficult

Eggs are laid one at a time, with the hen sitting on the nest an average of a about one hour per laying session for the first five eggs. (Gary Griffen photo)

to follow her. Hens sometimes fly the last 100 feet or so to the nest, probably to prevent being tracked by a predatory mammal. Some fly from the nest when leaving on recess. Incubating hens favor mid-morning and late afternoon for taking recesses and seldom are off their nests at high noon.

After about 25 days of continuous incubation, the eggs begin to hatch. The first sign of hatching comes when the poult in the first egg laid — which had been incubated the longest — begins to make peeping calls and starts to make a hole in its shell. In a few hours the other poults begin peeping and opening their shells.

The calls made by the hatching poults stimulate the brooding instincts of the hen, and the interaction between hen and poults begins "parental imprinting," a process by which the young poults learn that they are turkeys. Poults become imprinted on the first large,

moving object they see and hear upon hatching and, under normal circumstances, the first such object is the brood hen.

Parental imprinting provides the poults with the necessary motivation to follow the hen from the nest and to obey her vocal commands. During the nearly two days required for the brood to hatch, the poults learn to distinguish their mother's voice from the voice of all other turkeys and begin to recognize their siblings individually.

Parent voice recognition and imprinting of the chicks are not unique to the wild turkey. Imprinting was first observed in geese and described by the late Konrad Lorenz. It occurs in virtually all bird species that have large broods that leave the nest soon after hatching.

Poults open their egg shells at the large end, using a tiny "egg tooth" that will fall off a day or two after they

Preceding page — Each time an egg is laid, the hen covers it with dried leaf litter. In this way, nesting material collects as a result of egg-covering and not intentional nest-building. (Marcia Griffen photo)

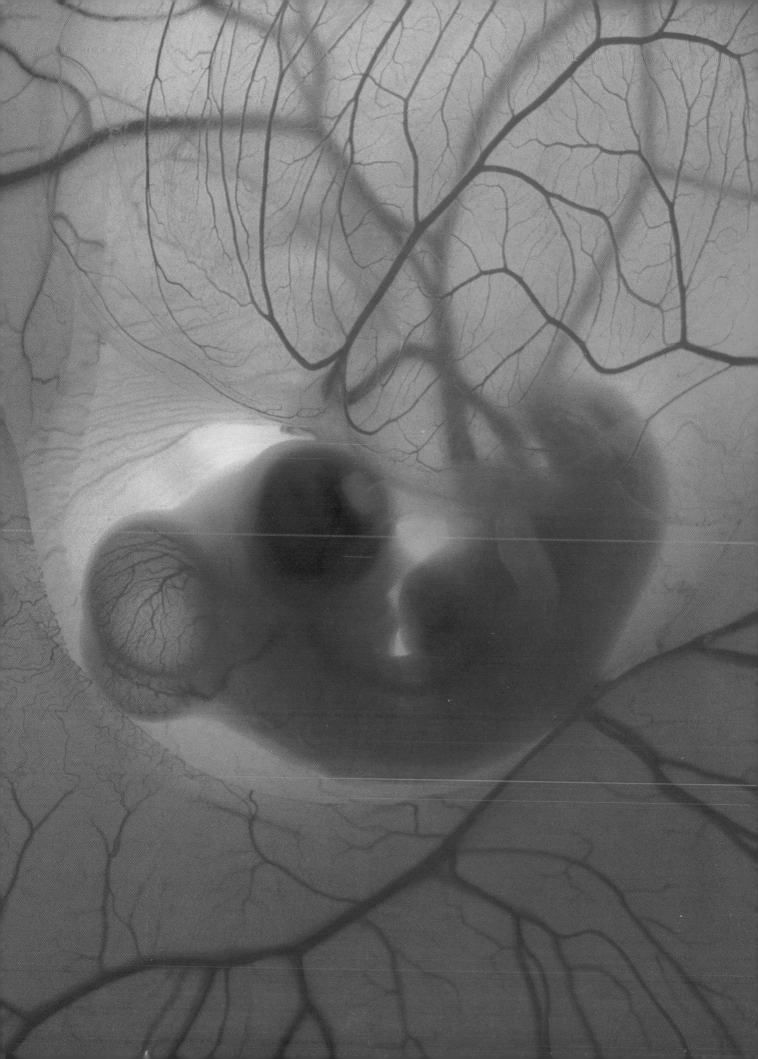

Photo courtesy the author.

Preceding page — *Clutches usually consist of 8 to 13 eggs, which require about 25 days of continuous incubation. This turkey embryo is in a middle stage of development. (Marcia Griffen photo)*

Following page — *During the incubation period, hens do not cover the eggs when leaving the nest to eat or to defecate. (Gary Griffen photo)*

The poult is coming out of its shell, a process that occurs from eight hours to two days after it makes a first small hole in the shell to obtain fresh air. (Gary Griffen photo)

This is followed in a few hours by the other poults in their respective laying succession. (Gary Griffen photo)

After hatching, the poult dries off from embryonic fluids and its feathers fluff out, leaving it looking less bedraggled and more like a bird. (Gary Griffen photo)

hatch. Predators peck holes or bite and crush the eggs into various shapes and pieces, making hatched egg shells, with their opening always at the big end, easy to distinguish from the remains of predated eggs.

Nest departure of the brood is probably triggered by the growing restlessness of the older poults as they approach two days of age. When the hen decides it is time to leave the nest, she yelps to the poults more frequently and more loudly than before, stands rather abruptly, and begins to walk slowly away. The poults that hatched first follow her closely. Sometimes the late-hatching poults linger in the nest, unable at first to choose between the warm nest and the hen moving away into a strange new world.

The hen will stop and continue to call to the reluctant poults. Her calling will finally coax them from the nest and to the source of the familiar voice. When all have joined the waiting hen, the new family flock will turn and resume its slow movement away from the nest, never to return. Left behind will be a silent cluster of empty egg shells in a shallow depression on the ground. In a day or two, a scavenger will ramble through and destroy the remains. The small spot on the ground that had been a center of secrecy, anticipation, creation, and anxiety will again become just another part of the field or forest.

Some birds, for example the northern bobwhite quail, are said to have a synchronized hatching process. This process causes all the eggs in a single clutch to hatch during a very brief period, even if some have been incubated longer than others. Supposedly, the sounds made by the first hatching quail chicks stimulate the others to hatch sooner. The wild turkey brood requires nearly two days to hatch and appear to have no such

Page 107 — The poult opens the top of the egg by pecking holes around the circumference, "can opener" fashion. (Marcia Griffen photo)

Page 106 — (Photo courtesy the author)

The whole brood usually takes about two days to hatch. (Gary Griffen photo)

hatching synchronization.

If a wild turkey hen is disturbed and abandons her nest when her eggs are still hatching or before the poults are adequately imprinted, the brood is doomed because the poults will not follow the hen or heed her vocal commands. When wild turkey eggs are hatched in incubators, the poults must be parent-imprinted on a turkey, substitute brood hen, or human during the first three or four days of life that imprinting can occur; otherwise, they will not imprint at all and will live their lives in a state of confusion, fearful of all large animals. Unimprinted poults never become really tame, regardless of how much human attention they are given.

Egg-eating predators such as raccoons, crows, opossums, and skunks destroy about one-half the turkey nests each season. A few nests are lost when especially heavy rains flood them, but late spring cold is probably not a serious cause of nesting loss — fresh turkey eggs can still hatch even after being lightly frozen.

Most hens that lose a nest will lay again a few days later in a new nest; some will renest as many as five times in a season if their nests are destroyed during the laying period. A hen is less likely to renest if she was incubating when the nest was destroyed. Second and third attempts at nesting in the same season are usually made within or near the same home range the hen used for the first attempt. If a hen successfully hatches a clutch, however, her nesting efforts conclude for that season.

A hen may nest in the same home range in successive years and occasionally will make her nest only a few feet from one of former years. One radio-tracked hen in Georgia nested in the very same spot in two suc-

Following spread — During the time required for the brood to hatch, the poults begin to recognize their siblings individually. (Gary Griffen photo)

109

Photo courtesy the author.

Following page — *The calls made by the hatching poults stimulate the brooding instincts of the hen, and interaction between the hen and poults begins. (Gary Griffen photo)*

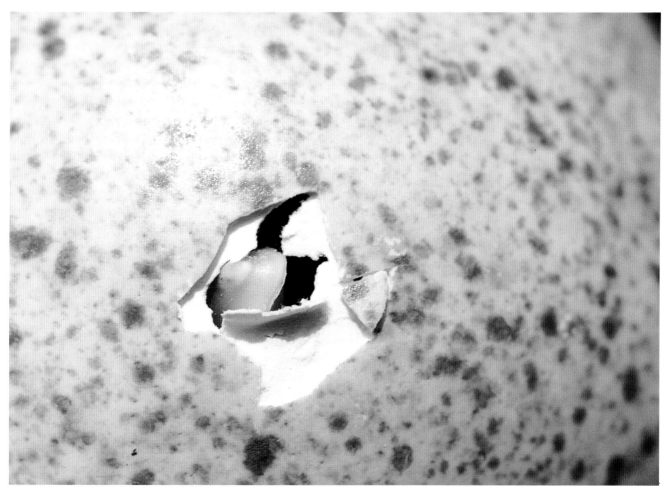

Poults open their shells at the large end, using a tiny "egg tooth" that will fall off a day or two after they hatch. This process is referred to as **pipping***. (Marcia Griffen photo)*

cessive years.

The annual molt of nesting hens is delayed until after they are through nesting for the season, which can delay the process, compared to the molting of gobblers and non-nesting hens, for instance, for more than a month. However, when the nesting hens do finally begin to molt, they replace their old plumage more rapidly than do other turkeys and finish plumage renewal in late fall, about the same time as the rest of the population.

Although the typical hen makes her nest, lays, incubates, and hatches her brood as I have described, not all conform to the mode. Innate genetic variation is expressed in the extraordinary differences that one sees in the wild turkey from bird to bird and place to place. Whether the behavior of the "typical hen" in our Florida studies is typical of wild turkeys everywhere will not be known until similar research is done elsewhere. My experience with wild turkeys warns that much variation will be seen before enough is known to detect the patterns.

The New Brood

The body weight of a turkey poult when it leaves its egg shell is about two ounces and does not increase appreciably during the first week after hatching. During this period it begins to feed by pecking at small insects and vegetation but receives most of its nourishment from a reserve of egg yolk which is still inside its abdomen. During the second week, as its hunting ability and digestive processes improve, its weight nearly doubles, and by the time the poult is six weeks old, it is carrying a pound in body weight and will continue to grow at a rapid rate during the rest of the summer.

Preceding page — Parental "imprinting" provides the poults with the motivation necessary to follow the hen from the nest and to obey her vocal commands. (Gary Griffen photo)

Photo courtesy the author.

Page 116 — *A turkey egg that has been predated by a crow. (Photo courtesy the author)*

Preceding page — *New turkey poult with egg tooth still visible. (Marcia Griffen photo)*

The wild turkey brood goes about its daily routine under the control of the hen's voice. (Gary Griffen photo)

Grown turkeys without broods roost in trees at night to evade prowling predators. Poults, however, are unable to fly at first and have to roost in weedy cover on the ground, under the body and outstretched tail and wings of the hen. This is an especially hazardous time for the brood — every predator in the woods will eat every young turkey it can find, and many will eat the hen. In studies conducted in Florida (Williams and Austin, 1988) and in Alabama (Speake, 1980), more than one-half the poults succumbed to predation during the two-week period of ground roosting. Some of the brood hens themselves fell to foxes, bobcats, large birds of prey, coyotes, and free-ranging dogs during this period. As serious as this predation appears, the ground-nesting turkey's losses are no greater than losses suffered by many birds that nest in trees. According to nature's design, the wild turkey's high rate of natural reproduction compensates for its high death rate.

The wild turkey brood goes about its daily routine under the control of the hen's voice. When danger threatens a flightless young brood, the hen utters a soft alarm call. This causes the poults to freeze instinctively, whether or not there is vegetation in which to hide.

If the poults are well hidden, the hen will often move away from the place they are hiding and will watch from a distance. If the disturbance threatens the poults, the hen will act as though injured or may feign an attack on the intruder, be it wild animal or man.

I have seen hens show only moderate concern when I was near a hidden poult, but show increasing alarm when I was moving away. Such behavior would confuse any predator that based its search pattern on the level of alarm exhibited by the hen.

After the disturbance subsides, the hen may continue

Following spread — When danger threatens a flightless young brood, the hen utters a soft alarm call, which causes the poults to freeze instinctively. (Gary Griffen photo)

Even as the poults grow older, the pattern of assembly is based on the call of the hen. (Gary Griffen photo)

to sound the "alarm putt" to silence the brood. When all appears safe, she will issue her call to bring the poults from hiding and to her side. She and the brood will then move quickly away from the area.

Even as the poults grow older, the pattern of assembly is based on the call of the hen. To assemble her brood, the hen will return very near the spot that an attack occurred, the place from which her call is most likely to be heard by all the poults. This behavior reveals that turkeys have little fear of a site where a predator attacked them, provided enough time has elapsed for the predator to move on.

Turkey poults gradually gain the ability to fly as their new wing feathers and muscles develop. When the brood travels, those that fall behind will hop over tree roots and fallen branches to catch up, and throughout the day will flap their wings and jump in pursuit of choice insects or to reach dangling ripe berries. By the time they are eight days old, poults can skip through the woods with the aid of their wings, barely touching the ground at all. Then the question of the "age of first flight" becomes more one of defining the term "flight" than a question of physical capabilities of the young birds.

For four or five days after the poults can fly a short distance, the brood will continue to sleep on the ground at night. Then, one evening near sundown, when the brood is two weeks old, the hen will fly to a low branch of a tree and yelp for the young to join her. One by one they will flutter up to her side and nestle under her wings for the night. I have not had the good fortune of witnessing a first-roosting flight myself. It must be a feat of some proportions for the hen to get all the brood on the same tree limb beside her.

Following page — This older poult has feathered out well and has shed its egg tooth. (Gary Griffen photo)

Turkey poults gradually gain the ability to fly as their new wing feathers and muscles develop, allowing them to roost in trees with the more mature birds in a flock. (Gary Griffen photo)

After once flying up at night, the poults will not roost on the ground again, nor will the hen until that becomes necessary again with next season's brood. A poult that survives the deadly fortnight of ground roosting may, with any luck at all, survive for another year.

Predation is the major cause of wild turkey deaths. Constant vigilance is the price of survival for the wild turkey throughout its life. If threatened by a predatory bird, one of the poults will sound an alarm call and the brood will dash under nearby trees and shrubs. If the danger is from the ground, the brood will "putt" and flush into nearby trees. When feeding in a lush meadow or field, a brood will remain within about 100 yards of woodland cover so it can fly into the trees if necessary.

Nature culls its flocks ruthlessly. Careless and inattentive wild turkeys do not survive long enough to pass on their fatal weaknesses to future generations.

Young turkey poults are sheltered on the roost by the body and partly opened wings and tail of the hen, and, in our studies in Florida, were not seriously affected by wet weather. In colder climates, exposure may be a more serious problem for turkeys. Disease, however, can cause losses of wild turkeys everywhere.

It is difficult to assess accurately the threat of disease because so little is known about the health of free-living wild turkeys. Turkeys affected by a debilitating disease are likely to be taken by predators as they weaken. Also, those that die of sickness without being captured by a predator are quickly eaten by scavengers and are rarely found in suitable condition for diagnostic examination.

"Blackhead" disease, or enterohepatitis, caused by the protozoan Histomonas meleagridis, is a well-known

***Preceding spread** — Sometimes a poult will roost on a hen's back. (Marcia Griffen photo)*

turkey disease. It has devastated domestic turkey flocks and has occasionally been reported in wild populations. It is spread by soil that is contaminated with the organism and by a small parasitic worm that carries the protozoan. Blackhead is not readily spread by flocks of true wild turkeys, which wander about extensively; many of the cases that have been reported were in relatively sedentary domestic or game farm turkeys that depended on feeding stations.

The symptoms of a disease called "fowl pox" are often mistaken for blackhead and probably account for many false reports of blackhead. Pox, caused by a virus and spread by biting insects, is commonly experienced by turkeys in their first summer of life, after which the birds develop an immunity to the disease. Death sometimes occurs from especially bad cases, however.

Wild turkeys suffer from several other poultry diseases and can tolerate many of them without serious ill effects. Like all wild animals, turkeys harbor some relatively harmless internal and external parasites. The large, flat lice commonly seen on wild turkeys live off fragments of feathers and shed layers of skin and do not bother the turkeys. Egg cases of these harmless lice are often found on the feathers under the turkeys' wings where the birds cannot reach when preening.

Following page — Nature culls its flocks ruthlessly. Careless and inattentive wild turkeys do not survive long enough to pass on their fatal weaknesses to future generations. Here, an Eastern coyote stands over a hen that will become its dinner. (Gary Griffen photo)

127

FOODS AND HABITAT

An animal species that specializes in eating only a few food items is at the mercy of environmental conditions that might cause a crop failure of its narrow diet. The wild turkey is in no such danger. Its broad and flexible diet enables it to occupy a wide geographic range and promotes relative stability in turkey population size from one year to another.

Turkey foods include almost everything that has nutritive value and is small enough for a turkey to swallow, but turkeys do show strong feeding preferences. Most food is swallowed whole; large items are sometimes picked into small enough parts to swallow.

Like many other seed-eating birds, the wild turkey has a large crop or "craw," like an elastic compartment, in its upper esophagus. The crop is where food is stored before it moves down the digestive tract. The digestive process is slow for hard seeds, so having a storage pouch enables the turkey to utilize large quantities of food, when found, even if its stomach is full. A wild gobbler's crop will hold nearly a pint of food weighing over one pound.

The turkey's stomach is a muscular gizzard that has strength sufficient to crack wild pecans and hickory nuts. Pecans swallowed whole require one hour for the gizzard to crush while hard-shelled hickory nuts take 30 hours or longer (Schorger, 1966). The turkey ingests small quantities of tiny stones, called "grit," to assist the gizzard in the grinding and crushing process, but some of the harder seeds, such as hickory nuts and seeds of flowering dogwood, serve the same purpose when retained in the gizzard.

Acorns, wild pecans, and other seeds of trees ("hard mast") that fall to the ground usually provide more food than the turkeys and other wildlife can consume in autumn. Fruits of trees and shrubs ("soft mast"), and seeds and flowers of herbs and grasses are also abundant. Fall is a time of plenty for turkeys.

The easy harvest continues into winter when many shrubs and vines still hold seeds in reach of the turkeys and there is an abundance of dormant insects, spiders, plant galls, buds, and winter berries. Food items left over from fall can still be scratched out of the forest litter and, in the moist places, especially in the South, there may be succulent green vegetation such as fern sprouts, green leaves, and plant bulbs. Cattle dung in pastures and fields contains fragments of grain and harbors insects that turkeys also seek out. Many cultivated grain fields still hold remnants of their crops, which provide additional sustenance for turkeys. In the South, some small edible understory plants begin to grow and bloom, even in winter, to take advantage of the sunlight coming through the leafless hardwood forest canopy. In winter in the South and in fall in the North, turkeys find ample food and become fat, achieving their maximum annual body weight.

Spring brings drastic changes to the woods. Trees and shrubs put on leaves that shade the understory vegetation, and although the trees bloom and produce fruit, the seeds are not mature and the trees hold on to them. Hungry turkeys may fly into trees to eat spring buds, but the nourishment received is inconsequential.

Following page — *Young male turkeys spend much of their time wallowing, preening, sunning and dusting. Dusting serves to eliminate lice and other parasites. (Gary Griffen photo)*

Photo courtesy the author.

The ground litter has been scratched through by almost every animal in the woods. Forest productivity, which depends on sunlight, is in the tree tops. The spring forest presents a bare cupboard at turkey level.

As feeding conditions worsen in the deep woods, turkeys shift their daily home ranges to feed in openings and forest edges that have begun to produce spring buds, flowers, fruit, seed, succulent leaves, and insects. By the time the broods hatch in late spring and early summer, forest openings and their edges, where direct sunlight reaches the ground, are producing abundant food.

More than 25 percent of the poult's diet is insect and other small animal life that is high in protein. Such food is not available in the shade of a mature deciduous forest. Wild turkey habitat with many openings and fertile fields in summer will produce the most poults and have the most turkeys.

Over most of the turkey's range, oaks are the most important food producers. The acorns they produce are found by the turkeys almost the year around. Acorns are not essential, however. In years of complete acorn crop failure, turkeys survive in good health on other foods. Other trees that make seed or fruit that contribute to the turkey's fall and winter diet are black cherry, black gum, hickory, hackberry, magnolia, pines, sweet gum, ashe, persimmon, cypress, sabal palm, American beech, and many others. These are especially important in areas with few or no oaks.

Food-producing understory trees and shrubs such as flowering dogwood, blue beech, hawthorns, hollies, and viburnums also produce turkey foods. In the

Preceding page — In many regions, flowering dogwood is the most highly preferred food item in the wild turkey's diet. (Photo courtesy the author)

Following page — Wax myrtle, or "bayberry" fruit is a late winter favorite of wild turkeys. (Photo courtesy the author)

woods' edges and ecotones are wax myrtle (bayberry), blackberries, and huckleberries. And there are food-producing vines such as wild grapes, poison ivy, roses, greenbriar, and honeysuckle in the woods and along the woods' edges.

The most valuable summer and early fall food plants are the grasses. Their seeds and leaves are as important in the warm seasons as acorns are in fall and winter and are critical for turkey brood-rearing.

Many other small weedy plants also produce foliage, flowers, fruit, or seed and harbor insects and spiders that turkeys eat. The list includes most of the ferns and mosses, stargrass, wild cucumber, sedges, buttercup, boneset, burdock, wild lilies, irises, water cress, vetches, partridge berry, asters, buttonweed, and hundreds of others. Altogether, the wild turkey is known to eat more than 600 different food items. The list will grow much longer as more studies are done.

Wild turkeys will pass up food items in one geographic area that are favorites somewhere else. When food scarcity occurs, they will fall back on secondary preferences to obtain the necessary nutrition. Variety in its habitat and flexibility in its feeding habits are the wild turkey's insurance against the uncertainties of nature.

Wild turkeys will drink water from streams and ponds, on occasion, but evidently do not need to drink often in humid climates where there is heavy morning dew and the vegetation contains ample water. However, lack of surface water is believed to limit the distribution of wild turkeys in the arid southwestern U. S. There turkeys are often found in close association with artificial water sources provided for cattle.

The wild turkey is a bird of the woodlands. It does not long thrive where there are too few trees, regardless of the amount of food available. The westward limit of the turkey's original range in the U. S. corresponds to the edge of the treeless Great Plains. There turkeys existed only along wooded streams. The turkey's dependence on woodlands is partly a reflection of its role as a prey species: It must have trees as overhead cover from soaring hawks, for safe roosting at night, and to fly up into to escape stalking predators.

The more the turkey is pursued by predators, natural or human, the greater is its need for deep woods. In places of few predators and little human molestation, turkeys can live in landscapes with relatively few trees. However, sizable expanses of large timber are important to turkeys for the seclusion cover that is needed when hunting pressure is heavy or when there is other intensive human disturbance.

As important as trees are to the welfare of the wild turkey, heavy timber alone does not make optimal turkey habitat. Dense forest is fall and winter range. The best wild turkey populations occur where the woods are laced with grassy fields and meadows and where there is a wide variety of cover types in the landscape. This includes openings, water courses, and different woodland types of varying timber densities.

Places where woods and grassy, open areas meet are especially attractive and beneficial to turkeys. The close proximity of these important types of habitat requires turkeys to travel only short distances to use one type or the other. Low annual movement equates with high-quality habitat, low levels of stress, and high population density. The advantageous situation of having cover types in close proximity, with vegetative transitions between them, is called the "edge effect" by wildlife ecologists.

Preceding spread — An example of excellent bottomland turkey habitat at Fisheating Creek in Glades County, Florida. (Photo courtesy the author)

Following page — The author checks a wild turkey nest site in cover that is nearly perfect for nesting and brood rearing. The brood that hatched here spent the entire summer within one mile of this nest site. (Photo courtesy the author)

CONCLUSION

The wild turkey is a highly adaptable, resourceful, and, at least for today, successful wild animal. Although its numbers may be increasing, its future is far from assured. The future of wildlife such as the wild turkey will be determined by the priorities of another animal we call man. If human populations continue to increase as they are now doing, there will be no room, except in zoos, for the wild turkey. Then there will probably not be enough room for even our own species.

It is already too late for many wild species. Many more, including the wild turkey, will disappear from Earth unless our values change drastically and quickly. People who do not like to think about such things are at the core of the problem.

****

With that said, let's wind down this turkey story on a more cheerful note. A good way to leave wild turkeys is on the roost as we found them in the opening pages, near the banks of Fisheating Creek.

In the late afternoon, after a day of foraging in the liveoak hammocks and pinewoods, the four old gobblers moved silently toward the cypress swamp. They stopped now and then to listen and to watch as a gentle breeze stirred the understory shrubs and grasses. One fell behind to pick and swallow a few large flower heads in a patch of wild iris and then trotted across the glade to catch up with the others. The four moved on into the cypress woods.

The great birds were near a favorite roosting place, but it was not quite time to fly up into the trees. A titmouse was singing and a red-shouldered hawk called in the distance. All heads snapped up to listen to a pileated woodpecker pounding a dead snag. Satisfied that all was safe, the gobblers turned in different directions to scratch among the moist leaves. They tarried there until the sunlight began to fade from the treetops.

At the moment of sundown there was still enough light in the shadows of the swamp for me to see the red of a cardinal airplant that was clinging to a nearby cypress trunk. Before long, though, all color would be gone from the swamp. It was already difficult to see one of the gobblers as he moved out of sight behind a clump of buttonbush. From behind the vegetation he croaked a coarse, two-note yelp, and the others quickly answered.

Then, as suddenly as it had left its roost in the morning, one of the gobblers burst into the air from behind the buttonbush, climbed at a steep angle, and landed in a cypress tree. As he spread his wings for balance, a second gobbler flew up noisily and landed in another tree. A minute later all four were on their roost in the cypress swamp again, each in a separate tree, hardly a stone's throw from last night's roost.

I could hear the wings of another flock flying to roost across the swamp. A hen was yelping loudly, but the old gobblers paid no attention.

The old turkeys changed limbs to find the one most suitable for the night. Then they stood and calmly preened their plumage, occasionally looking up and

Preceding page — Two mature toms, ready for mating before females come into season, display on a warm, late winter day. (Gary Griffen photo)

139

around the area. All four peered down into the swamp to spot the source of a suspicious sound. A deer rustled by. Then, satisfied there was no danger, the gobblers again buried their bills in their feathers and resumed preening.

The barred owls across the creek gave out their caterwauling calls and were answered by the lone hoot of another from farther down the swamp. A pair of sandhill cranes gave their clattering calls in the distance as a night heron passed overhead, sounding its brusque squawk. The sounds of day were giving way to the sounds of night.

One of the gobblers squatted on his tree limb, his tail jutting squarely beneath, then stood suddenly and craned his neck downward for a long minute, straining to see some animal shuffling under the roost. Then, one by one, the gobblers silently squatted on their tree limbs and settled for the night.

In the western sky, where the sun had already set, the fading semi-circle of dim, pinkish light slipped lower, becoming weaker by the second. The frogs that had been mostly silent by day were chirping again and there was more to hear than to see in the swamp.

The sun was gone for another day from the swamps and glades, and the turkeys of Fisheating Creek were asleep.

Preceding spread — Wild turkey gobblers in the dim light of a cypress swamp. (Photo courtesy the author)

SUGGESTED READING

Bland, Dwain. 1986. Turkey hunter's digest. DBI Books, Inc. Northbrook, Illinois. 256 pp.

Bevill, V. W. 1973. Some factors influencing gobbling activity among wild turkeys. Proceedings of the Annual Conference of Southeastern Association of Game and Fish Commissioners. 27:62-73.

Leopold, A. S. 1959. Wildlife of Mexico. University of California Press, Berkeley, California. 568 pp.

Moby, H. S., and C. O. Handley. 1943. The wild turkey in Virginia: its status, life history and management. Commission of Game and Inland Fisheries, Richmond, Virginia. 281 pp.

Potter, Thomas D., Sandford D. Schemnitz and William D. Zeedyk. Status and ecology of Gould's turkey in the Peloncillo Mountains of New Mexico.

Speake, D. W. 1980. Predation on wild turkeys in Alabama. Pages 86-101 in J. M. Sweeney, ed. Proc. fourth national wild turkey symp. Natl. Wild Turkey Fed., Edgefield, South Carolina.

Williams, L. E., Jr. 1966. Capturing wild turkeys with alpha-chloralose. J. Wildl. Manage. 30:50-56.

Williams, L. E., Jr. 1981. The Book of the Wild Turkey. Winchester Press, Tulsa, Oklahoma. 181 pp.

Williams, L. E., Jr. 1989. The Art and Science of Wild Turkey Hunting. Real Turkeys Publishers. 331 pp.

Williams, L. E., Jr. and David H. Austin. 1988. Studies of the Wild Turkey in Florida. University Presses of Florida, Gainesville. 232 pp.